Extraordinary WOMEN in POLITICS

Extraordinary WOMEN *in* POLITICS

by
Charles Gulotta

Children's Press®
A Division of Grolier Publishing
New York   London   Hong Kong   Sydney
Danbury, Connecticut

This book is dedicated to Maria,
my very favorite extraordinary woman.

Visit Children's Press on the Internet at:
http://publishing.grolier.com

Library of Congress Cataloging-in-Publication Data
Gulotta, Charles
Extraordinary Women in Politics / by Charles Gulotta
    p. cm. (Extraordinary people)
Includes bibliographical references and index.

Summary: Presents biographical sketches of women who have been influential in the world's political arenas throughout history.

ISBN 0-516-20610-9 (lib. bdg.)   0-516-26399-4 (pbk.)
1. Women in politics—Biography—Juvenile literature. [1. Women in politics. 2. Women—Biography.] I. Title. II. Series.
HQ1236.G85 1998
322'.082—dc21
[B]   97-37186
                                                                                        CIP
                                                                                        AC

Contents

11 Introduction

17 The Ancient World

19
Cleopatra VII
69–30 B.C.
Queen of Egypt

24
Isabella I
1451–1504
First Queen of
a Unified Spain

28
Catherine de Médicis
1519–1589
The Power behind
the Throne

32
Mary, Queen of Scots
1542–1587
A Lifetime of
Royal Problems

35
Catherine the Great
1729–1796
Powerful Empress
of Russia

39
Sojourner Truth
c. 1797–1883
U.S. Abolitionist

42
Woman's
Suffrage

51
Elizabeth C. Stanton
1815–1902
Tireless Crusader
for Women's Rights

54
Susan B. Anthony
1820–1906
A Lifetime of Devotion
to Women's Causes

58

Queen Victoria
1819–1901
Six Decades on the
Throne of England

74

Jeannette Rankin
1880–1973
First Woman in
the U.S. Congress

92

Sirimavo Bandaranaike
1916–
First-Ever Woman
Prime Minister

63

Tz'u-hsi
1835–1908
A Half-Century
of Power in China

79

Eleanor Roosevelt
1884–1962
Expanding the
Role of First Lady

96

Indira Gandhi
1917–1984
First Woman Prime
Minister of India

66

Queen Liliuokalani
1838–1917
The Last Queen
of Hawaii

84

Margaret Chase Smith
1897–1995
First Woman Elected to
Both House and Senate

101

Ella Grasso
1919–1981
First Woman Governor to
Get There on Her Own

70

Aleksandra Kollontai
1872–1952
A Voice for
Russian Women

88

Golda Meir
1898–1978
First Woman Prime
Minister of Israel

105

Eugenia Charles
1919–
First Woman Prime
Minister in the Caribbean

109

Eva Perón
1919–1952
First Lady
of Argentina

126

Jeane Kirkpatrick
1926–
First Woman U.S. Ambassador
to the United Nations

143

Nancy Kassebaum
1932–
Groundbreaking
Senator from Kansas

114

Bella Abzug
1920–1998
A Fighter All the Way

131

Violeta Barrios de Chamorro
1930–
First Woman President
in Central America

147

Corazon Aquino
1933–
First Woman President
of the Philippines

118

Shirley Chisholm
1924–
First African-American
to Run for President

135

Sandra Day O'Connor
1930–
First Woman Supreme
Court Justice

151

Madeleine Kunin
1933–
First Woman
Governor of Vermont

121

Margaret Thatcher
1925–
Solid Leadership
in Shaky Times

140

Vigdis Finnbogadottir
1930–
Europe's First
Woman President

155

Ann Richards
1933–
First Woman
Governor of Texas

159

Jane Byrne
1934–
First Woman
Mayor of Chicago

176

Barbara Mikulski
1936–
Maryland's Champion
of the Working Class

192

Carol Moseley-Braun
1947–
First African-American
Woman in the Senate

163

Edith Cresson
1934–
France's Fighting
Prime Minister

180

1992: Year of
the Woman

196

Madeleine Albright
1937–
First Female
Secretary of State

168

Geraldine Ferraro
1935–
First Woman Vice
Presidential Nominee

184

Dianne Feinstein
1933–
Tough and Sensitive
Mayor and Senator

200

Gro Harlem Brundtland
1939–
Norway's Champion
of the Environment

173

Barbara Jordan
1936–1996
First African-American Woman
to Preside Over a Legislature

188

Barbara Boxer
1940–
Women's Advocate in
the House and Senate

204

Patricia Schroeder
1940–
Twelve-Term
Congresswoman

208

Mary Robinson
1944–
One of Ireland's
Bright Lights

222

Tansu Çiller
1946–
First Woman Prime
Minister of Turkey

240

Benazir Bhutto
1953–
First Woman Prime
Minister of Pakistan

211

Wilma Mankiller
1945–
First Woman Chief of
the Cherokee Nation

226

Hillary Rodham Clinton
1947–
The Most Influential
First Lady

244

Activists

214

Christie Todd Whitman
1946–
First Woman Governor
of New Jersey

231

Olympia Snowe
1947–
Maverick Senator
from Maine

247

Gloria Steinem
1934–
Author, Publisher,
Activist

218

Hanna Suchocka
1946–
Strong, Resilient,
Courageous

236

Kim Campbell
1947–
First Woman Prime
Minister of Canada

251

Aung San Suu Kyi
1945–
Civil Rights
Leader, Myanmar

255

Bernadette Devlin McAliskey
1947–
Northern Ireland's
Civil Rights Leader

259 Women in World Politics

265 Important Dates in Women's Political History

270 Organizations and Online Sites

276 For Further Reading

278 Index

288 About the Author

Introduction

*E*xtraordinary *Women in Politics.* The very title seems to demand that such a book exist. Especially now, at the end of a century in which women have made such dramatic progress in politics—a century that gave us Golda Meir, Margaret Thatcher, Corazon Aquino, Eleanor Roosevelt, and so many others. What better time to issue an encyclopedia of the most notable?

And yet, even as we celebrate the subjects of this book and their many accomplishments, we cannot avoid taking at least a brief look at what remains to be done. If a woman can lead Great Britain, Israel, or Nicaragua, for example, why couldn't one lead the United States? If a woman can become prime minister of the Philippines during violent and uncertain times—and safely stay in power—why couldn't the same thing happen in Rwanda? Or Myanmar? Or even Kuwait? Why can't a woman be elected to high office without having to endure questions about her appearance, her favorite recipes, or her husband's financial dealings? And if a woman can be elected to the highest office in a nation's government, why can't that government put an end to the widespread violence, poverty, and discrimination afflicting the rest of that nation's women?

When women were universally excluded from the political process, their problems remained invisible to the rest of the general public. The gender that represented half the world's population had almost no representation in government, and therefore no way to make itself heard on a national level. Over the past hundred years, women have gradually won the right to vote and hold elected office in countries all over the globe. The results of that process have been largely positive. Unfortunately, success has a way of blurring vision. Many people seem to believe that because women now have a voice in government, all their problems have been solved. On the contrary—while women have won seats at virtually every level of government, they still account for a relatively small percentage of elected officials. They therefore enjoy less than their share of political power, and their ability to effect change remains limited.

Given the magnitude of the struggle, it seems doubly appropriate to discuss the lives and achievements of those women who have served as pioneers on the political frontier. But before we can honor those women, we must first decide who they are. Specifically, what is our definition of politics? Must a politician be elected to office? Is a judge involved in politics? A secretary of transportation? A queen?

The dictionary definition describes a politician as anyone involved in the conduct of government. That's much too ambitious, obviously. Such a job description would have to include congressional pages, lobbyists, secret service agents, and receptionists. To qualify for inclusion in this book, the person had to directly affect public policy, change the system as a whole in some positive way, or improve political opportunities for other women.

Some simply had to be included for the book to be worthy of its own title: the already mentioned Meir, Thatcher, and Aquino, for example. These women were chosen to lead by the people of their nations. What, then, of Eleanor Roosevelt? She was never elected to public office. On the other hand, she affected public policy and actively fought for numerous political causes—

before, during, and after her years as First Lady. Likewise, Susan B. Anthony was never elected to any office of government. But her work in winning the right to vote for American women made it possible for countless others to hold office.

Okay, so who is extraordinary? Many of the women in these pages accomplished things that were extraordinary because of where they took place. In the United States and other industrialized nations, people now take for granted a woman's right to vote and hold elected office. But go back to the year 1900, and the only women in the world who could vote lived in Wyoming, Colorado, Utah, Idaho, and New Zealand. No woman, in any country, could hold elected office before the twentieth century. Even today, girls growing up in some Arab nations can only dream about having a voice in national or even local government. And in places all over the world, women who can vote and hold elected office cannot enjoy the benefits of those rights, because they are too busy struggling against poverty, violence, and discrimination in jobs, housing, and health care. Under such circumstances, it is that much more difficult to gain any kind of political footing. That is why some of the women in this book are here just because they got elected. What they actually did in office becomes secondary. Their most important accomplishment was convincing enough voters—male and female—to trust the judgment and abilities of a woman, because that newfound trust opens the door for all women in the future.

Other women have been included because of the timing of their accomplishments. A woman getting elected to the house of representatives in California in 1996 did not necessarily accomplish something extraordinary. A woman getting elected in Montana in 1916 definitely did. In some fields, a person is deemed extraordinary for a single feat, even though it may have taken years to accomplish. Neil Armstrong, for example, has done many admirable things, but he is known primarily as the first person to walk on the moon. Similarly, the first person to achieve something in politics may be extraordinary for the "pioneer" aspect of the accomplishment. Violeta Chamorro was the first woman elected president of Nicaragua. Regardless of her actions in office, her election was a remarkable achievement. The same goes for Sandra Day O'Connor. Her record may be no more impressive than that of her fellow Supreme Court justices. But she is counted as extraordinary because she was the first woman to sit on that court.

Very often, especially in politics, a person may give many years of service without ever achieving a "first walk on the moon," or any other single outstanding success. That person's accomplishment is a long period of consistently good work, and some of those women are included here as well, such as Bella Abzug, Shirley Chisholm, Pat Schroeder, Olympia Snowe, and Barbara Mikulski.

What about those who were not included? There are fifty-five women whose lives are described in this book. For each one, there are several more who could have been added, each with her own remarkable story. In the end, it came down to a simple, unavoidable truth: there isn't room for everyone. The decision was, at times, arbitrary. Could Lucretia Mott have been substituted for Elizabeth Cady Stanton? Of course. But then we'd be discussing why Mott was in and Stanton was not. Hopefully, the sampling of women in this book paints a fairly accurate picture of the history and the current status of women in politics.

Are these people perfect? Hardly. A few have been brilliant leaders. Some have been absolutely ruthless. Many have been caught up in scandal. All have made mistakes. But such is the nature of politics, and politicians. Women have proven that, as leaders, their best is every bit as good as men's. And their worst is just as bad.

As you read through the book, you may be surprised now and then. For example, did you know that women in Poland won the vote (1918) before women in the United States (1920)? Were you aware that many societies are matriarchal—that is, women provide the driving force that makes those societies function—yet they do not treat women as equal to men in the political arena? Looked at another way, the men in those countries can tolerate their grandmothers being boss of the family but cannot imagine her as boss of the government. In other places, citizens can accept women serving as queen, but not as president, prime minister, or head of the military.

You may be surprised, also, by the hardships so many of these women had to endure. We tend to believe, especially in America, that anyone with enough money can succeed in politics. But it takes more than money. For some, it takes a willingness to risk everything. Read about Benazir Bhutto's struggle to become prime minister of Pakistan, even though her father, himself a former prime minister, had been jailed, tortured, and finally hung. Imagine what Dianne Feinstein must have felt as she took over as mayor of San Francisco, just hours after her predecessor was assassinated in his own office. Take note of how many of these women lost parents and siblings at a very early age, how many went through divorce and defeat, violence, poverty, and imprisonment. Think about what these woman learned as children and experienced before they came to power, and you may begin to rethink the labels we all so casually slap on our political leaders.

Then look at the history of women's fight for political equality around the world, and you may begin to understand how slowly change takes place. Women have had the vote in New Zealand and Australia for almost a hundred years. Yet, neither nation has ever elected a woman to a major government position, and in 1994 neither had more than 22 percent female representation in any house of parliament. According to the United Nations

Report on the Fourth World Conference on Women, issued in 1995, "on average, women represent a mere ten percent of all elected legislators worldwide." What makes that interesting is the fact that virtually every nation on earth has more women than men. In 1984, Geraldine Ferraro ran for vice president of the United States. She is still the only woman who has ever been considered seriously for the job.

This brings up another significant point: the process of changing a society is never smooth or consistent. It is a series of forward steps, unexpected curves, detours, backward steps, more forward steps, and so on. All during that time, which may involve years, decades, or centuries, people will discuss the situation. They will yell in anger, and sometimes act with violence. They will look back and say things were better before. They will demand change now. They will proclaim what must be done next. They will try to predict the future. Almost always they will be wrong. For the truth is, no matter where we sit in space or time, we can only see a little way ahead.

Perhaps by reading about the people in this book, we will be able to see just a little farther. What will we ask our future leaders to do about hungry, illiterate, and abused children? Will we make real progress in our effort to develop societies in which people are not mistreated because of their sex, skin color, or religion? Will we find alternatives to war?

In the new century, we may begin to discover the answers to some of these questions. Or we may find ourselves more confused than ever. One thing is certain: change will continue. And with that change will come many more extraordinary women in politics.

The Ancient World

*I*n the world of ancient Greece, around 500 B.C., hundreds of city-states dotted the region around the Mediterranean Sea. The territory controlled by ancient Greece stretched from present-day France to the Black Sea, and as far south as the northern coast of Africa. The city-states may have had populations ranging from several hundred to several thousand.

Within the city-state, the rights granted to citizens and noncitizens, men and women, varied widely. The rights of female citizens, for example, exceeded those of slaves of either sex, but never approached those granted to male citizens. A female citizen was protected by law from being kidnapped or sold into slavery. Women could take legal disputes to court, but had to be represented by men. In fact, every woman was required to have a male guardian, who protected her physically and legally. Women could neither vote nor attend political meetings. Their role was to organize and run the household: care for the children, supervise the slaves, prepare food, weave cloth, and keep the family's finances in order.

Around the same time in Egypt, women enjoyed a social and legal status that was nearly equal to that of men. Women could purchase and sell property, initiate lawsuits, and become educated. Some historians believe that Egyptian women even received equal pay for equal work.

The king of Egypt was considered a divine being who served as a connection between his subjects and the gods. As the absolute ruler, the king saw that justice was carried out, and he was responsible for keeping order, both in society and nature. Unlike the supernatural gods, however, the earthly kings had power that could be taken away. And when no male heir was available, a female could become queen. So it was possible—even somewhat common—for women to assume the throne.

In some ancient cultures, women held religious authority. They were revered as shamans in parts of Asia, for example, and as high priestesses in Rome. The worship of goddesses was common, and there is evidence that certain societies were matrifocal (female-centered). But even in those cultures, the average woman had fewer rights than the average man. She was expected to be obedient and productive. Those who showed rebellious or independent tendencies were often branded as witches, prostitutes, or demons.

With the rise of monotheistic (single-god) religions, women were further relegated to positions of weakness and inferiority. As the Roman Empire spread over Europe, North Africa, and parts of the Middle East, it brought with it the belief that women had to be feared, worshiped, and protected. The notion of equality with men did not surface until the eighteenth century.

Cleopatra VII

Queen of Egypt
69–30 B.C.

The name Cleopatra brings to mind adventures set in an exotic and ancient land. She was queen of Egypt at a time when three great civilizations were intertwined. She mingled with the likes of Julius Caesar, Marcus Antonius (usually known as Marc Antony), and other historical figures who now seem larger than life. She has been the subject of plays, books, sculptures, and paintings. For these reasons, we tend to remember only the legends. But the truth is thrilling enough, for Cleopatra influenced the course of history.

Actually, there were several Egyptian queens named Cleopatra. The most famous, Cleopatra VII Philopator, was born in 69 B.C. in Alexandria, near the mouth of the Nile River. She was the daughter of Ptolemy XII, or Auletes, the ruler of Egypt. The father of Auletes, Ptolemy XI, had expressed in his will that Egypt should become part of the Roman Empire, but Rome was suffering from corruption and disorganization. In 60 B.C., the three Roman rulers, Julius Caesar, Marcus Crassus, and Pompey, joined forces to get things running smoothly again. In 59 B.C., Auletes went to Rome and paid off the three with money and gifts. In return, they convinced Rome's Senate to declare Egypt an ally of the Roman Empire. However, the Egyptian people were angered by the secret deals, and Auletes fled the country. His two elder daughters, Cleopatra VI Tryphaena and Berenice assumed control. When Cleopatra VI died soon after, Berenice claimed the throne for herself.

Auletes was not out of the picture, however. He was in Rome, looking for help. When Berenice learned of this, she sent "representatives" to get in his way. Auletes had them murdered. After more bribery and scheming, Auletes returned to power in 55 B.C., with the aid of a Roman cavalry led by a military commander named Marc Antony. Auletes immediately had Berenice executed. Four years later, Auletes died, and Cleopatra VII ascended the throne with her brother, Ptolemy XIII. She was eighteen years old, and he was fifteen.

Cleopatra was intelligent, ruthless, courageous, and skilled in politics. She also knew the value of communication and was fluent in numerous languages. But speech couldn't help her deal with the famine of 48 B.C., when the Egyptian harvest failed and people became restless for change. Ptolemy XIII was a minor and ruled with the aid of an advisory council. These advisers took advantage of the current difficulties, gained Ptolemy's loyalty, and drove Cleopatra from power. She fled to Syria, raised a strong army, and returned to fight.

Meanwhile in Rome, Crassus had been killed in battle, and Caesar and Pompey were building armies against each other. Their confrontation took place in 47 B.C., with Caesar winning easily. Seeking safety, Pompey and his

soldiers left for Egypt—just as Cleopatra was about to attack her brother's ruling council. The Egyptians decided to welcome Pompey into their midst, then kill him, in order to pacify Caesar. And that's what they did. Within days, Caesar arrived in Alexandria and was presented with Pompey's head. But Caesar demanded money and a meeting with Cleopatra and Ptolemy XIII. Afraid of her brother, Cleopatra wrapped herself in a rug, sneaked into the palace, and met Caesar. The two fell instantly in love. The next morning Caesar arrested Ptolemy, whose advisers responded by attacking Caesar's forces. They were defeated in battle, and Ptolemy was killed. Cleopatra's younger sister, Arsinoë, who had also turned against her, was banished to Rome.

Caesar and Cleopatra celebrated their victory aboard an enormous pleasure ship on the Nile. When Caesar returned to Rome, Cleopatra stayed in Egypt to rule unopposed. She soon gave birth to Caesar's son. Then, on March 15, 44 B.C., Caesar was assassinated by sixty senators who believed he was planning to establish a monarchy in Rome. Devastated by Caesar's death and paranoid about her situation in Egypt, Cleopatra ordered the murder of her brother, Ptolemy XIV, even though the young boy posed no threat to her.

By 42 B.C., Marc Antony had emerged as the sole ruler of Rome. When he summoned Cleopatra to his palace, Antony fell in love with the Egyptian queen, just as his predecessor had. Cleopatra asked for the murder of her sister, Arsinoë, which was quickly carried out. In Alexandria, the two rulers staged long celebrations. In 40 B.C., Antony left Cleopatra to address military matters. The next year she gave birth to twins, a boy and a girl. In 37 B.C. Antony and Cleopatra staged a wedding ceremony, although he had at least two other wives. Antony gave back to his latest bride much of the land her forefathers had controlled. In 36 B.C., Cleopatra gave birth to her fourth child, Ptolemy Philadelphus. Antony was engaged in a disastrous battle in Parthia, near present-day Iran. Having survived that adventure, Antony returned to Alexandria, where he and Cleopatra made plans to finish conquering the entire Mediterranean.

Octavius, Caesar's adopted son, had other ideas. He launched a verbal campaign against Antony, describing him as a lovestruck traitor who planned to treat Alexandria as the center of the Roman Empire. The two sides assembled their forces and met at sea in the Battle of Actium, where Antony made the mistake of repeatedly accepting Cleopatra's military advice. When she retreated from the battle in her flagship, he abandoned his soldiers and followed her. In Alexandria, with Octavius's forces approaching the city and thinking Cleopatra had committed suicide, Antony killed himself with his own sword. Cleopatra feared that she would be taken prisoner by Octavius and paraded through the streets of Rome for public ridicule. According to lore, the queen of Egypt allowed herself to be bitten by a poisonous snake and died on a bed of gold.

Cleopatra had caused, or at least influenced, the downfall of two of the world's most powerful leaders. She had altered the interaction among the world's three most dominant civilizations. And she had sown the seeds of legend.

Isabella I

First Queen of
a Unified Spain
1451–1504

For several centuries, Spain and Portugal had been a collection of kingdoms. Within those kingdoms, groups of Christians, Jews, and Muslims lived separately but competed for control. From the twelfth to the fourteenth centuries, the Christians gradually gained dominance, spreading their influence over most of the peninsula. But Spain was not truly united as a nation until the late 1400s, when a queen named Isabella I and her husband, Ferdinand II, captured the last remaining Muslim stronghold. In that same year, 1492, the Christian monarchs also expelled the Jews from Spain and sent an Italian navigator across the Atlantic Ocean in search of a new route to the Orient.

Isabella was born on April 22, 1451, in Madrigal, Castile, Spain's largest kingdom. She was named after her mother, Isabella of Portugal. Her father was Juan II, the longtime ruler of Castile. When Juan II died in 1454, his son from a previous marriage assumed the throne as Enrique (Henry) II. Meanwhile, the widowed and powerless queen was forced to live in her castle at Arévalo, raising Isabella and her younger brother, Alfonso. Isabella was tutored by nuns and priests. Her only friend was a girl about her age named Beatriz, who was the daughter of the castle's governor. When Isabella was eleven, Enrique called for her and Alfonso to come live with him at the castle. Beatriz joined them.

Enrique was not well liked among his subjects. He had few morals and did not display the strength and courage his people wished for. Trust was in short supply at the castle. Plots were continually hatched by one group against another. Enrique made promises, then broke them. He ignored pleas and protests from the many people in the kingdom who had suffered injury or injustice. And he declared Alfonso rightful heir to the throne, then seemed to change his mind. These circumstances provided Isabella with her first real experience of a ruling monarchy. She was not impressed.

Gradually, resentment turned to violence, and civil war broke out. The rebels organizing against Enrique wanted to replace him with Alfonso. In 1467, the armies met in battle, but no clear winner emerged. The following summer, a plague hit the region, and Alfonso, at the age of fourteen, became ill and died within a day. Those who had supported Alfonso now encouraged Isabella to fight for the crown. She declined. Hoping to restore peace, she chose to simply wait her turn. But when Enrique suddenly issued an order for Isabella's arrest, she fled to the north.

Isabella, now in her late teens, had been trying to reach her cousin Ferdinand, who was heir to the kingdom of Aragon in eastern Spain. She wished to marry him, because she knew their marriage would someday unite the country. The couple had never met, but they knew a great deal about each other. When they finally met and became acquainted, their feelings grew quickly into love. On October 18, 1469, Isabella and Ferdinand were married, four days after they first met. Before the wedding, they had signed an agreement that would keep control of Castile, the largest of Spain's kingdoms, in Isabella's hands. Ferdinand would acquire limited authority.

In early December 1474, Enrique collapsed suddenly and died. The next morning Isabella was crowned in the great square in Segovia. Her enemies, led by the king of Portugal, quickly launched an attack. But the Spaniards had organized a large army, and with Ferdinand and Isabella right in the thick of the fighting, the Portuguese were easily defeated.

Queen Isabella truly cared about the people of Castile. She worked to restore law and order to the region. She took away a great deal of authority from the noblemen, making herself more powerful. And she helped end the long period of scandal. Still, for most of the 1480s, Ferdinand and Isabella were at war with the Moorish kingdom of Granada in southern Spain. On January 2, 1492, the king and queen captured Granada, and Spain was at last one nation.

Under Isabella's rule, Spain was transformed. She provided for a set of laws to be written, organized, and enforced consistently throughout the land. She established a permanent army. Spain became a major center of international trade. The ancient feudal system of lords, nobles, and serfs was severely weakened, making way for a new and important middle class. But religious persecution also flourished under Ferdinand and Isabella after they introduced the Spanish Inquisition in 1480.

Under the Inquisition, the Catholic Church tried to identify Jews who had converted to Catholicism simply to avoid punishment. Thousands were jailed or executed. In 1492, the Jews were officially expelled from Spain. Later, the Inquisition turned its attention to Muslims and Protestants.

The year 1492 was also significant for another reason. For many years, a navigator named Christopher Columbus had been trying to win royal support for an expedition. He believed he could reach India by sailing west across the Atlantic Ocean, but he needed funds to prove it. Refused by the kings of England and Portugal, Columbus turned to Ferdinand and Isabella. Columbus convinced the royal couple to support his effort. By March 1493, he had returned to their castle to describe some of the vast and rich lands he had claimed for Spain. A century of Spanish exploration and dominance in the New World had begun.

Isabella died on November 26, 1504. She was buried at the cathedral in Granada. During her last years, she saw three of her children die. She was succeeded to the throne by her third child, Juana. The youngest, Catherine, later married Henry VIII, king of England.

Catherine de Médicis

The Power behind
the Throne
1519–1589

Her father died five days before Catherine was born. Her mother died two weeks after giving birth. Catherine grew up in the care of her uncle, who was the pope, an aunt, a group of nuns, and a great-aunt. By fourteen she was married. She learned Greek, mathematics, astronomy, and hunting, and many other things not familiar to the average sixteenth-century woman. But Catherine de Médicis was far from average. For three dramatic decades she was the most powerful woman in her nation. She was mother to three successive kings of France. Thousands of their subjects were killed at her command, even as she preserved a monarchy in danger of disappearing.

Catherine de Médicis was born on April 13, 1519, in Florence, Italy. Her father was Lorenzo de' Medici, the Duke of Urbino. Lorenzo was the last male descendant of the Medici family, which had long ago established a financial dynasty in Europe. Lorenzo's uncle was Giovanni de' Medici, also known as Pope Leo X. Realizing that the permanence of the family name and position was at stake, Leo arranged for Lorenzo to capture Urbino, a small Italian state, and become its duke. The pope then arranged a marriage between Lorenzo and Madeleine de la Tour d'Auvergne, a wealthy French heiress. With Madeleine pregnant and less than a week before the baby was due, Lorenzo died. After Catherine's birth, her mother developed a fever and within two weeks was dead. Now the family was on the edge of extinction. Its fate would rest in the hands of a scheming pope and a helpless infant.

Catherine was cared for by an aunt in Florence. Leo X died suddenly in 1521. A year later he was replaced by Giulio de' Medici, known as Pope Clement VII. From 1527 to 1529, Catherine stayed in a series of convents until 1530, when she went to Rome to live with a great-aunt. There, Pope Clement VII began his plan to match Catherine, now eleven, with the Duke of Orléans, in France. Three years later, on October 28, 1533, they were married in Marseilles. Fourteen years later, the duke ascended the throne of France as Henry II.

Outside the palace, the world was changing. Capitalism was growing, while the Catholic Church crumbled into many smaller parts. Catholics persecuted Protestants. Higher taxes were issued. War and revolt raged for many years. By 1559 Spain had emerged as the strongest power in Europe. France had lost land, men, money, and much of the respect it had cherished.

Catherine gave birth to ten children between 1544 and 1556, seven of them surviving infancy. Then, at the end of June 1559, Henry was wounded in a jousting tournament and died. His oldest son, Francis, was fifteen. Legally he was old enough to serve as king, but emotionally he was unprepared. When a monarch is unable, because of emotional immaturity or physical disability, to fulfill the duties of the throne, a regent is named to carry out those responsibilities. Catherine was named regent. Her goal was to keep the monarchy afloat, even as the waves of change crashed against the palace gates. Francis II was king for little more than a year: he died in 1560. Next in line was Charles, age ten, who became Charles IX. Again, Catherine controlled the throne and ruled as regent.

Religious war broke out between Catholics and Protestants in 1562. Catherine worked hard to restore peace and to keep the crown safe from those who would take its power. Her son had little interest in ruling, and the Catholics saw his weakness as a chance to gain influence for their side. Catherine designed the Edict of Tolerance, announced by the government in 1562 as an attempt to reduce the conflict. Essentially, the law legalized both religions in France. It satisfied no one, and all sides were somewhat critical of its neutral approach. War erupted again in 1568. Once more, in 1570, Catherine restored calm by issuing the Peace of Saint-Germain, which gave Protestants additional liberties. But two years later, Catherine discovered that the Protestants were gaining influence over Charles. She convinced Charles that the Protestants were a threat to the government and had to be eliminated. What followed has come to be called the St. Bartholomew's Day Massacre. On August 24, 1572, some twenty thousand people were killed throughout France. In one move, Catherine had lost the trust of both the Protestants and the Catholics.

Charles IX died in 1574 and was succeeded by his brother, who became Henry III and ruled for the next fifteen years. Confident in Henry's abilities, Catherine gave up her power as regent and became an effective ambassador for the king. Meanwhile, she negotiated with the Catholic League, whose power still threatened the stability of the monarchy. And she continued to support the arts, as she had done throughout her life. Through her efforts, a new wing was added to the Louvre Palace (now a world-famous museum in Paris), the Tuileries gardens were constructed, and various châteaux were built. Her personal library was widely known in part for the many rare manuscripts it housed. Catherine, who outlived seven of her ten children, died at Blois on January 5, 1589.

Mary, Queen of Scots

A Lifetime of
Royal Problems
1542–1587

Billions of people have walked this earth, but few have had lives filled with more drama, heartache, intrigue, death, and betrayal than the woman known as Mary, Queen of Scots. Mary ascended the throne as queen of Scotland when she was less than a week old. She became both queen of France and a widow before her eighteenth birthday. Her second husband grew jealous of her secretary, an Italian man, and had him murdered before Mary's very eyes. From there, life began to get difficult.

Mary Stuart was born at Linlithgow Palace in Scotland, on December 8, 1542. Her parents were Mary of Guise and James V, king of Scotland. When James V died six days after Mary's birth, and a year after the deaths of his two legitimate sons, the infant girl became queen. There was a great deal of competition and conflict among those adults assigned to carry out Mary's responsibilities. In July 1548, a marriage was arranged between Mary and Francis, heir to the throne of France. She sailed to France the following month and for the next ten years was raised in the style of French nobility.

Mary and Francis married on April 24, 1558. Fifteen months later Francis ascended the throne when his father, King Henry II, died suddenly. Then, in December 1560, Francis himself died. Mary's mother had died in June of that year, and it was decided that Mary should return to Scotland to become queen. However, the situation wasn't much neater in Mary's homeland. Scotland was ruled by a collection of Protestant lords, most notably James, Lord Stewart, who was also Mary's half-brother. The lords were often in conflict with the Protestant clergy, a source of turmoil that required both firmness and flexibility from the throne. As queen, Mary did her best to satisfy her various advisers, as well as the Protestant and Catholic churches, while also ruling effectively.

In July 1565, Mary married Lord Darnley, her first cousin and a Roman Catholic. The Protestants were enraged by the marriage and started a rebellion, which came to an abrupt end when Mary herself went out to face the protesters. Within a short time, Lord Darnley (or Henry, as he was known) proved himself to be an inadequate ruler and was all but cut out of the authority loop. As the emotional distance between the royal couple increased, Mary went looking for support. She found it with David Riccio, her secretary. This period of mild comfort was not to last, however. In March 1566, Riccio was murdered at Holyrood Palace, in Mary's presence, by a group of

Protestant lords. The plot was likely hatched by Henry himself. Mary, six months pregnant at the time, gave birth to a son in June. He would become James VI of Scotland and, later, James I of England.

By the end of the year, Mary was trying to end her marriage. Conveniently, Henry was murdered in February 1567. His death was surrounded by mystery, but it was believed by some to have been connected to Mary's growing relationship with the Earl of Bothwell. By May, Bothwell had been acquitted of murder charges, and two weeks after his own divorce, he and Mary were married.

Meanwhile, Mary's public and private support had steadily crumbled. As her new husband fled, she was imprisoned in July 1567 and forced to abdicate. Mary's son became King James VI of Scotland. Aided by her remaining friends, Mary escaped from prison and convinced a large force to fight for her. The group was badly defeated, however, and Mary headed for England to seek support from its queen, Elizabeth, who was Mary's cousin.

Elizabeth did little. She refused to punish Mary yet was unwilling to help her. Nineteen years passed, and many conspiracies by Roman Catholics and foreign agents swirled around Mary during much of that time. Finally, she was found guilty of plotting to assassinate Elizabeth. Reluctantly, the queen issued the order for Mary's execution, and on February 8, 1587, she was beheaded. Mary is buried in Westminster Abbey.

Catherine the Great

Powerful Empress
of Russia
1729–1796

They called her an immoral, power-crazed tyrant who had murdered her husband. But this sophisticated German princess became ruler of the largest empire in Europe. She never learned to master the Russian language, yet she helped turn the University of Moscow into a world-renowned center of learning. She ruled for more than thirty-four years, acquiring vast territories for the country. And in the end, they called her Catherine the Great.

Sophia Augusta Frederika was born princess of Anhalt-Zerbst in Stettin, Germany (now Szczecin, Poland) on April 21, 1729. Her father, Christian

August, was prince of Anhalt-Zerbst, and her mother, Johanna, was princess of Holstein-Gottorp. Despite the impressive titles, neither parent had money, and August fought in the Prussian army as a freelance soldier. Johanna was determined to have a son, so after Sophie was born, she quickly became pregnant again and gave birth to Wilhelm. Sophie was all but cast aside, first in the excitement of a male heir, and then in the care Wilhelm required for a severe leg deformity. Another brother, Frederick, was born when Sophie was five, and still another died in infancy.

The princess, meanwhile, was an energetic, precocious child who could read French before age four. She was curious about everything and loved to learn. Yet she received little acknowledgment from her mother and was the object of frequent physical discipline. Her greatest offense, in her mother's eyes, was that she was not pretty.

In 1742, Wilhelm died. Three years later, Sophie was baptized in the Orthodox Church and christened Catherine Alekseyevna. Some time later, Catherine was betrothed to her cousin, Peter, heir to the throne of Empress Elizabeth of Russia. Catherine did not enter the engagement with complete confidence. There were many strict laws that kept women enslaved to the church and to their husbands. Wives were frequently beaten for no other reason than to keep them obedient. If they died from such abuse, the husbands were not punished and were free to marry again. No less important, Catherine did not find Peter especially attractive or enjoyable to be with. Nevertheless, the wedding took place on August 21, 1745, followed by a nine-day celebration. The next seventeen years were mostly unpleasant for Catherine, who had to endure not only her husband's numerous shortcomings, including frequent drunkenness and infidelity, but the mad whims of his aunt, the empress.

Catherine's chief responsibility was to provide an heir to the throne. After nine difficult years, the future Paul I was born in 1754, although serious questions about the boy's true father were never settled. Perhaps because of her own childhood, Catherine rarely showed her son affection or acknowledged his strengths.

On December 25, 1761, Elizabeth died and Catherine's husband assumed the throne as Emperor Peter III. His reign was to be short, however, as Peter was almost universally hated, a sentiment shared most strongly by Catherine herself. Peter's actions after coming to power were largely self-serving and did little or no good for Russia. On June 28, 1762, after months of careful planning, a plot to overthrow him was carried out, and Catherine, with the blessing of the church, was declared empress. For the next week confusion reigned. Then, on July 6, Peter was killed by one of his guards. It was widely suspected that the execution had been ordered by Catherine, and many of her subjects feared she was a power-hungry murderer.

Catherine assumed power over a country torn apart by poverty, famine, and violence. Her rule, many believed, would be short and ineffective. But Catherine had given years of thought to how Russia should be governed. Thoroughly prepared, she set to work immediately. She was up early every morning, consulting with advisers, reading reports, and issuing directives. Catherine restored to the senate legislative powers taken away by her late husband. She established direct communication with each provincial governor and military commander so that she would know of each region's problems and progress. And she listened to advice before taking action. The empress was inspired by Peter the Great, czar at the beginning of the eighteenth century, who had instituted many reforms beneficial to Russia. Yet she ruled with the insecurity of knowing she might be overthrown at any moment. Her many love affairs involved men wishing to share—or steal—her power. "I want the laws obeyed," she wrote in her journal. "But I want no slaves. My general aim is to create happiness without all the whimsicality, eccentricity, and tyranny which destroy it."

During Catherine's reign, Russia acquired large portions of Poland. Long years of war with Turkey brought more land and made the empress a national heroine. Schools increased in number and quality, farms were modernized, and the arts flourished. A workable system of justice was established. Tax burdens were eased. Swamplands were drained and built into towns. With a growing population to develop and protect its vast territories, and with an increasingly organized system of government, Russia was becoming a dominant nation. And despite frequent peasant rebellions and conflicts with the church, Catherine was generally worshiped and respected. Her intellect, thoughtful reforms, and obvious devotion to Russia earned her the title, Catherine the Great.

In August 1796, Catherine suffered a stroke that left her extremely weak. She continued to rule somewhat effectively until November 5, when she was found unconscious on the floor of her room. She died the next day, setting off a period of mourning, followed by burial in the Cathedral of Peter and Paul in St. Petersburg. Perhaps in an effort to heal a national wound, or maybe just as an act of revenge, Catherine's son and successor, Paul I, had the body of Peter III reburied next to hers.

Sojourner Truth

U.S. Abolitionist
c. 1797–1883

As a girl and young woman, Sojourner Truth had several names and several masters. She had come into the world a slave, her mother's twelfth child to either die or be sold into slavery. She was sold four times, never learned to read or write, and was thirty years old before she tasted freedom for the first time. During the Civil War she shook hands with President Abraham Lincoln, and by the time she died, she had become something of an American legend.

Sojourner Truth was born near the end of the eighteenth century in the town of Hurley, about midway between New York City and Albany. Her original name was Isabella Baumfree, and she was later named Isabella

Hardenberg. One of her masters married her to a slave named Tom, and the couple had at least five children. She later claimed to have had thirteen children, "and seen them almost all sold off into slavery, and when I cried out with my mother's grief none but Jesus heard."

As a young woman, Isabella sought comfort in religion, a haven she took with her wherever she went. In 1827, she managed to escape to freedom and spent the next year in hiding. That same year, New York state officially abolished slavery. Isabella took two of her children and headed for New York City to try to get work as a domestic. There she became involved with a religious cult, which eventually disbanded.

In 1843, when she was about forty-six, Isabella said the voice of God told her to take the name "Sojourner" and to travel far distances to show people the sins of their ways. She said God gave her the second name "Truth" because her mission was to speak the truth, especially about slavery. With little more than twenty-five cents and a bag of old clothes, Truth left New York City and traveled across Long Island, and then up into New England, preaching, singing, and attracting large audiences. In Massachusetts, she met some of the most prominent abolitionists of the era and quickly won their respect. More than six feet tall with a deep voice, Truth possessed a commanding presence, even though she did not have an educated command of the English language. She became a well-known speaker because of her passion, her music, and her ability to express difficult ideas in simple ways, and she could quote extensively from the Bible, which she had memorized. Truth spent the next twenty years lecturing on slavery and women's rights. In order to pay her way, she sold copies of *The Narrative of Sojourner Truth*, a book she had dictated.

At the outbreak of the Civil War in 1861, Truth raised money and gifts for African-American soldiers and continued to speak out against the evils of slavery. During one trip to Washington, D.C., she met with President Lincoln.

In 1862, Truth settled in Arlington, Virginia, where she worked to help former slaves find jobs and housing and adjust to a life of freedom. After the war ended, she tried to obtain land for freed slaves in the Midwest and strongly supported the idea of a black state.

Truth devoted the rest of her life to fighting for the rights of African-Americans and women. Shortly after the Civil War, she found herself waiting for a horse-drawn car on a Washington road. Congress had outlawed segregation in 1865, but on this particular day, several drivers passed her by. Finally, Truth stood in the middle of the road, forcing the next car to stop. When the conductor tried to force Truth out of the car, she refused. To increase public awareness of the new desegregation law, she had the man arrested and fired. Thus she became the nation's first "Freedom Rider," a full century before the bus boycotts of the 1960s.

Sojourner Truth died on November 26, 1883, in her home in Battle Creek, Michigan. More than a thousand people gathered for her funeral. They came to honor a woman who had won her own freedom, and who had shared that prize with many others.

Woman's Suffrage

THE UNITED STATES AND GREAT BRITAIN

The word *suffrage,* in the most general terms, refers to the right of an individual to vote in elections and to run for office. *Woman's suffrage,* therefore, refers to women's right to vote and run for office.

In 1789, the U.S. Constitution granted the vote to white males who were American citizens and at least twenty-one years old. (In various places and at various times, other requirements further reduced the number of people eligible to vote. These included the ownership of property, the ability to read and write, and the payment of a poll tax at the time of voting.) In 1870, the Fifteenth Amendment to the Constitution said that the right to vote could not be denied because of a person's race or skin color. A full fifty years later, the Nineteenth Amendment gave all adult women the right to vote and run for office. That law was passed by Congress in 1920, but was really the result of a century of work by hundreds of women with almost no political power.

Meanwhile, women in Great Britain were fighting for the same rights on their side of the Atlantic. As early as the fifteenth century, a few British women were petitioning for suffrage, but very few men or women took their efforts seriously. In 1792, Mary Wollstonecraft Godwin wrote *A Vindication of the*

This young English girl promotes the cause of women's suffrage in 1890s London. The placard depicts Mr. John Bull (the British equivalent of Uncle Sam) and his wife, who tells her husband, "We should get on better, John, if I rode a horse of my own," alluding to women's self-determination.

Rights of Women, in which she demanded that women be granted the right to vote. Five decades later, a reform movement consisting of workingmen included woman suffrage in its list of demands to Parliament. The Chartists, as they were known, failed to achieve their goals, but their efforts helped focus national attention on the women's movement.

In 1865, the National Union of Women's Suffrage Societies was formed, led by Millicent G. Fawcett. Two years later, by an act of Parliament, women taxpayers won the right to vote in local elections. The movement progressed steadily, despite opposition from many powerful leaders—including Queen Victoria and prime ministers William Gladstone and Benjamin Disraeli. In 1897, several groups merged to form the National Union of Woman Suffrage Societies. Six years later, a small subgroup decided the National Union was too polite and broke away to form the Women's Social and Political Union. This latter group engaged in boycotts, bombings, window-breaking, and harassment of lawmakers opposed to their cause. Suffragists were often jailed and fined for their actions. In 1913, one woman sacrificed her own life as a gesture of protest when she threw herself in front of racing horses at a derby.

During World War I, the British suffragists devoted their skills and organization to the war effort. In so doing, they finally won the support they needed from the general public and Parliament. Women over age thirty gained the vote in 1918. Ten years later, the age was lowered to twenty-one, matching the requirement for male voters. In 1929, Margaret Bondfield became the first female cabinet member in British history.

Back in the United States, the woman's suffrage movement ran a course similar to that in Great Britain. The first success probably occurred in Massachusetts. There, adult female landholders could vote in local elections from 1691 until about 1780, when stricter requirements once again excluded

U.S. suffragists protest outside the Metropolitan Opera House in New York City, in a photograph taken in 1919.

women. Several groups, including the Quakers, advocated suffrage for women throughout America's colonial period. However, antifeminist feelings were very strong among men—and not enough women were willing or able to organize into a political force.

During the early nineteenth century, women became heavily involved in other social reform efforts. These included the temperance movement, which tried to get laws passed banning alcoholic beverages, and the Abolitionist movement, which worked to outlaw slavery in the United States. However, resistance against women was so powerful, even within these movements, that woman's suffrage saw little progress. At the 1840 Anti-Slavery Convention in London, for example, well-known American feminists Elizabeth Cady Stanton and Lucretia Mott were forced to sit behind a curtain and were not permitted to address the participants.

The first women's rights convention met in 1848 in Seneca Falls, New York. Stanton and Mott were the leaders of that event, which sparked an angry and sometimes violent response across the United States. During the years following the convention, it was common for meetings featuring women speakers to be disrupted by threats and violence.

By the time the Thirteenth Amendment was ratified in 1865, formally abolishing slavery, the women's rights and abolitionist movements had gone their separate ways. The abolitionists wanted to focus on winning the right to vote for the freed male slaves, and feared involvement in the women's struggle would hurt their chances. In May 1869, Stanton and Susan B. Anthony formed the National Woman Suffrage Association. Its goal was a federal law granting all American women the right to vote. Six months later, another group led by Lucy Stone and Henry Ward Beecher founded the American Woman Suffrage Association. That group's plan was to win the vote state by state. In fact, the territory of Wyoming led the way by passing a women's suffrage law that same year. The two groups merged in 1890 to form the National American Woman Suffrage Association. Its members worked to get the vote for women on both the state and federal levels. As a result of their efforts, Colorado granted suffrage to women in 1893. Utah and Idaho did so in 1896, and over the next twenty years numerous states and territories followed suit. The Nineteenth Amendment was passed by Congress in

1920. It says, in part, that "the right of citizens of the United States to vote shall not be denied or abridged by the United States or by any State on account of sex."

In 1893, New Zealand passed the world's first women's voting rights act that did not require the ownership of property. In other words, any woman in New Zealand who met the age and citizenship requirements could vote in local and national elections. The next year, South Australia gave women the right to vote and the right to be elected to the state parliament. In 1899, Western Australia granted women the vote in state elections. And in 1902, Australia gave all white women over the age of twenty-one the right to vote and hold office in national elections.

These were breakthroughs. The two island nations in the Southern Hemisphere had taken a major leap forward as far as women and politics were concerned. A few years later, the world caught up, and passed, Australia and New Zealand.

In 1901, Australia ended decades of rule by Great Britain, becoming an independent commonwealth. Even so, Queen Elizabeth II of England is still considered Australia's head of state. She is represented in Australia by a governor-general. But the real head of government in Australia is the prime minister. No woman has ever served as either governor-general or prime minister of Australia. After winning the right to hold national office in 1902, the first women were not elected to Australia's parliament until 1943. That year, Dorothy Tagney took her seat in the upper house, and Enid Lyons was elected to the lower house.

New Zealand's record has been similar. Women there could stand for national office as of 1919. It took fourteen years to get women into the lower house, when Elizabeth McCombs and Mary Dreaver were elected in 1933. The upper house remained all-male until Mary Anderson's entry in 1946.

EUROPE

Scandinavian nations were the European pioneers for women's voting rights in the early twentieth century. Women in Finland were granted the right to vote and hold office in 1906. Norway followed the next year. Denmark and Iceland granted women the vote in 1915 and were soon followed by Iceland, Sweden, Poland, the Soviet Union, Luxembourg, Germany, Great Britain, Ireland, the Netherlands, and Czechoslovakia.

In many countries, women won the vote just before, or just after, the end of World War II. These included France, Italy, Bulgaria, Hungary, and Romania. Switzerland gave women the vote in 1971. In Liechtenstein, woman's suffrage did not arrive until 1984.

AFRICA

With most of Africa under the dominance of European nations such as Belgium, France, and Great Britain, suffrage had little chance of making an appearance until the middle of the twentieth century. The first cracks in the wall of all-male rule began to show in South Africa. There, in the Orange Free State, white women were given the vote in municipal elections in 1914. By 1930, white women could vote on an equal basis with men throughout South Africa.

Throughout the continent of Africa, however, black women and black men were excluded from the political process. Around the middle of the twentieth century, many of the British, Belgian, and French colonies in Africa gained their independence. Ghana, for example, working toward freedom from British rule, gave women the vote in 1950. The former French West

Africa granted universal suffrage in 1956, shortly before that nation separated into several independent republics. Morocco and Tunisia followed suit three years later.

ASIA

In many parts of the vast Asian continent, strict religious beliefs have hampered the ability of women to improve their social and political status. But change did come, slowly, during the period between the two world wars. In Burma (now Myanmar), for example, some women could vote as early as 1922, though universal suffrage was not achieved until 1935. Women in Thailand won the vote in 1932, followed by Turkey in 1934, and the Philippines in 1937.

In India, women could vote in seven of nine provinces by 1929. Five years later, Ceylon (now Sri Lanka) established equal voting rights. Women in Japan won the vote in 1946, followed by China in 1947 and Korea in 1948. Indonesia and newly independent India granted it in 1949. Pakistani women first voted in national elections in 1956, as did Cambodian, Vietnamese, and Laotian women.

In the Middle East, religious traditions delayed the arrival of woman's suffrage. Egypt gave women the vote in 1956, followed by Lebanon in 1957 and Iran in 1963. Many other Middle Eastern nations granted limited suffrage during the 1960s, often imposing restrictions on women not imposed on men. In 1998, women in Kuwait still had not ever voted. The nation of Israel, however, offered universal suffrage from its inception in 1948.

LATIN AMERICA

Women's suffrage gained a foothold in Central and South America shortly after World War I. It grew substantially after women won the vote in the

United States in 1920. Three years later, Mexican women voted in state elections for the first time. In 1927, Argentinian women won the right to vote in certain provincial elections. Then in 1928, Esther Neira de Calvo of Panama created the Inter-American Commission of Women, and through its efforts, women throughout Latin America began to make dramatic gains, largely thanks to de Calvo, Bertha Lutz of Brazil, Isabel de Vidal Urdenata of Uruguay, and Minerva Bernardino Coppa of the Dominican Republic. In 1929, Ecuador granted universal suffrage to women in national elections. Uruguay and Brazil followed in 1932, Cuba in 1934.

During and after World War II, women in Latin America were granted the right to vote in national elections on the same basis as men: the Dominican Republic (1942), Guatemala (1945), El Salvador and Panama (1946), Argentina (1947), Costa Rica and Chile (1949), Mexico (1953), Colombia (1954), Honduras, Nicaragua, and Peru (1955), and Haiti (1957).

Elizabeth Cady Stanton

Tireless Crusader
for Women's Rights
1815–1902

Elizabeth Cady Stanton grew up in a time when the activities of women were severely restricted. They could not file for divorce, even if their husbands were abusive. They could not vote or run for public office. They could not attend the better colleges and universities. They had little or no control over their own property. Their employment opportunities were few, and their pay was inferior to that of men, even for the same job. They were required to wear certain, rather restrictive, clothing in public. Most women recognized these obstacles and found ways to cope. Stanton saw them as challenges, and attacked them head-on.

Elizabeth Cady was born in Johnstown, New York, on November 12, 1815. She was somehow admitted to Johnstown Academy, a boys' school, but thereafter found most doors to higher education closed to her. Cady graduated from the Troy Female Seminary in 1832. She wanted to advance to law school but had to settle for studying law with her father, Judge Daniel Cady.

Unhappy with the social and institutional rules inhibiting women, Elizabeth joined the temperance and antislavery movements. She expected those activities to bring her into contact with people who shared her way of thinking but was shocked to find more of the same discrimination and injustice against women. She and a group of women delegates traveled to London for the world antislavery convention in 1840, but because of their gender had to sit behind a curtain, out of view of the speakers and the audience.

That same year, Cady married Henry Stanton, a noted abolitionist. The ceremony was completed, however, only after the word "obey" had been deleted from the bride's vows. The couple lived in Boston for the next six years, promoting the causes of temperance and abolition. They moved to Seneca Falls, New York, in 1847. A small town, especially when compared with Boston, Seneca Falls provided stark evidence of the limits placed on women, especially in education and employment. The evidence was all the more obvious to Elizabeth Cady Stanton, whose stalled ambitions had already fueled her anger and who was clearly ready for a fight.

On July 19, 1848, Stanton, Lucretia Mott, and other women assembled for the Seneca Falls Convention. That meeting officially began the women's movement in the United States. Stanton read the Declaration of Sentiments, modeled after the Declaration of Independence, which outlined the women's chief complaints and identified their objectives. For the most part, the women present wanted equal opportunities in work and education. Stanton convinced them to add the right to vote to that list. Three years later, she joined forces with Susan B. Anthony, and the movement had its leaders.

In 1869, Stanton and Anthony founded the National Woman Suffrage Association, and Stanton was elected its first president. The two women traveled the country, writing, lecturing, and distributing petitions to local politicians. They testified before legislative bodies and helped form local chapters of their organization. And they began publishing a weekly newspaper, *Revolution,* which carried the masthead: "The true Republic—Men, their rights and nothing more; Women, their rights and nothing less." In 1890, Stanton was elected president of the newly formed National American Woman Suffrage Association.

Although considered a radical, funny to some and dangerous to others, Stanton was in many ways a traditional woman. She married at twenty-five, raised seven children, and maintained a model home. She was, by most accounts, intelligent and charming and had a delightful sense of humor.

Stanton published a great deal, including *The History of Woman Suffrage* (1881–1886), which she coauthored with Anthony and Matilda Joslyn Gage, and *The Woman's Bible* (1895). In 1898, she published an autobiography, *Eighty Years and More.*

Except for an occasional victory, such as women gaining the right to vote in Wyoming Territory in 1869, Stanton saw few of her objectives become reality. The country was not ready for the changes she wanted, but Stanton had accelerated the process tremendously. She died on October 26, 1902, in New York City.

Susan B. Anthony

A Lifetime of Devotion to Women's Causes 1820–1906

For the first half of Susan B. Anthony's life, thousands of African-American women worked as slaves. They were treated as nothing more than property, with few rights and almost no personal freedom. Anthony fought hard to change that. By the time slavery was abolished in the mid-1860s, Anthony had found her calling: improving the status of *all* American women. She spent the second half of her life devoted to that cause. Today, her very name is a symbol of women's struggle for the right to vote and run for public office.

Susan Brownell Anthony was born in Adams, Massachusetts, on

February 15, 1820. She grew up on a farm near Rochester, New York. Anthony's parents were Quakers, and they encouraged her natural sense of independence, a trait that would shape the rest of her life. She entered the teaching profession, but quickly grew dissatisfied and returned to work on the family farm. The move opened up a new world to Anthony. Her parents' home was a meeting place for a wide variety of people interested in social reform, and Anthony took advantage of the opportunity to learn as much as possible. Her friendship with Elizabeth Cady Stanton, whom Anthony met in 1851, turned into a lifelong working relationship.

Anthony's exposure to the beliefs of men such as William Lloyd Garrison and Frederick Douglass instilled in her the conviction that she could, and should, become an advocate of change in American society. She first acted on those beliefs by speaking out in support of the temperance movement. However, her efforts met with unexpected resistance. By 1852, she had received such negative reaction from male temperance workers, who resented a woman trying to join their ranks, that she decided the primary need for reform was in the area of women's rights. Assembling a small group of like-minded acquaintances, Anthony formed the Woman's State Temperance Society of New York.

Anthony took her campaign across the state and then around the country. She spoke out for a woman's right to own property, to maintain custody of children after divorce, and to vote in state and national elections. Her approach often involved flooding a politician's office with thousands of signed petitions. In 1866, she helped found the American Equal Rights Association in an effort to give the movement a base and some organization.

When the Fourteenth Amendment to the Constitution was ratified in 1868, it guaranteed the vote to all male citizens at least twenty-one years of age. Anthony protested the restriction, arguing that women were citizens and

Elizabeth Cady Stanton and Susan B. Anthony posed for this photograph around 1881, while both were leading the National Woman Suffrage Association.

should be able to vote. In 1869, she helped establish the National Woman Suffrage Association. Many people laughed at her ideas. But in 1872, Anthony managed to register and cast a vote in Rochester. She was arrested, tried, and fined. (She refused to pay the penalty, explaining that the law was unjust and that the Fourteenth Amendment should apply to all citizens.)

By 1869, Wyoming had given women the vote in territorial elections. That same year, the women's movement split into two factions. One group advocated a constitutional amendment that would grant all American women the right to vote. It also addressed a variety of women's rights, including those concerning divorce and employment issues. The other group, calling itself the American Woman Suffrage Association, focused solely on the vote and held that individual states should handle the matter separately. Anthony and Stanton joined forces on the side of amending the Constitution, with Stanton becoming the first president of the National Woman Suffrage Association (1869–1890). When the two organizations merged, Stanton was elected president of the National American Woman Suffrage Association (1890–1892). Anthony succeeded Stanton, serving from 1892 to 1900.

Anthony died on March 13, 1906, in Rochester. Fourteen years later, the Nineteenth Amendment was passed, granting full suffrage to women. Many people called it the Anthony Amendment.

Queen Victoria

Six Decades on the Throne of England 1819–1901

During the early nineteenth century, the British Empire included vast territories on every continent. Britain was in every respect a world power. The monarchy of Great Britain, however, had been crumbling for many years. George III, king for five decades, was blind and senile. He rarely left his room in Windsor Castle. His seven sons were unpopular and did little to encourage public respect for the monarchy. Their unpleasant traits resulted in unhappy marriages, few children, and unlikely prospects for succession to the throne. Despite such gloomy circumstances, one son would eventually produce an heir. She would be queen for sixty-four years, the longest reign in the history of Great Britain. During her rule, she would redefine the role of the monarchy, influencing the policies of numerous parliamentary governments. And she would cause an entire nation—no, an entire empire—to fall in love with her.

Alexandrina Victoria was born in London's Kensington Palace on May 24, 1819. She was the only child of Edward, duke of Kent, and Louisa Victoria, princess of Saxe-Coburg. When Victoria was eight months old, her father died. A few days later, George III was also laid to rest, and his eldest son, George IV, became king.

Victoria's childhood was a lonely one, spent mostly with her overprotective mother. But Victoria was well educated and learned to find companionship in her books. She became fluent in English, German, French, and Italian. She was also skilled in music and art and began keeping a journal when she was thirteen. She would continue these activities for the rest of her life. From her tutors and her books she learned a great deal about the world. And from her loneliness she developed a strong sense of independence and solid values. She knew, even as a teenager, that her time as queen was not far off.

When George IV died in 1830, his brother, William IV, became king. When William IV died seven years later without any legitimate heirs, his niece Victoria ascended the throne. It was June 20, 1837, and she was eighteen years old. She wrote in her ever-present journal, "I shall do my utmost to fulfill my duty towards my country; I am very young and perhaps in many, though not in all things, inexperienced, but I am sure that very few have more real good will and more real desire to do what is fit and right than I have."

Victoria spent much of the next two years under the guidance of her prime minister, Lord Melbourne. He taught her the ways of politics, and she developed a strong affection for him. But Victoria's romantic feelings were reserved for her cousin, Prince Albert of Saxe-Coburg. She proposed to him on October 15, 1839 (it would have been improper for a prince to ask a queen), and they were married four months later.

Victoria was immensely happy after her marriage to Albert, with whom she had nine children. She trusted and respected Albert, and he helped balance her political views, yet she kept him in his place. Victoria did not share the monarchy with Albert, and he struggled to understand his role. Gradually he became indispensable to Victoria, handling the details of her life as queen.

In 1850, Victoria broke with tradition when she challenged the authority of the foreign secretary. The monarchy had always served in the role of adviser. Now Victoria insisted that the queen should be consulted on foreign policy matters. The foreign secretary ignored the queen's request and was eventually fired by the prime minister. But he had been a popular political figure in Britain, and the confrontation hurt Victoria in the eyes of her subjects. Her popularity fell even further in 1854, when she tried to keep her nation out of the Crimean War, a long and costly conflict between Turkey and Russia. When Britain's involvement in the war became inevitable, the queen gave it her full support. During the war, Victoria was active in organizing relief services for wounded soldiers. In 1856, she created the Victoria Cross, which has become Britain's highest award for wartime service.

When Albert died in 1861, Victoria began a period of mourning that would last the rest of her life. The queen was forty-two years old, a widow with eight unmarried children. She was devastated, yet she carried on, inspiring her subjects with a strong will and devotion to duty.

Queen Victoria's reign spanned twenty different parliamentary governments. She did not appreciate the company, or the politics, of most of the prime ministers. She found William Gladstone, prime minister on four different occasions, particularly disagreeable. Among other things, she opposed his goal of legalizing trade unions, as well as his policy of home rule for

This engraving, reproduced from a drawing by R. J. Lane, depicts Victoria soon after her ascent to the throne.

Ireland. She did work well with Benjamin Disraeli, who served as prime minister in 1868, and then from 1874 to 1880. It was Disraeli who secured for Victoria the title of empress of India. Victoria also supported the marquess of Salisbury, who held the office three times between 1885 and 1902. Victoria agreed strongly with both men in their attempts to protect and increase British interests throughout the world.

In 1887, Great Britain celebrated Victoria's jubilee (fifty years on the throne), and in 1897 her diamond jubilee. On those and numerous other occasions, her subjects flooded Victoria with adoration and devotion. She returned the feelings. Victoria died, surrounded by her family, on January 22, 1901. She was laid to rest beside Prince Albert. Their eldest son, Edward VII, was crowned king. Their descendants, including more than forty grandchildren, would marry into nearly every one of Europe's royal families. And the longest reign in British history would forever be known as the Victorian Age, a time of strong nationalism and conservative morality.

Tz'u-hsi

A Half-Century of Power
in China
1835–1908

Throughout history, there have been powerful political leaders who have abused their positions and committed horribly criminal acts to advance their own interests. There have been equally powerful heads of state who have used their authority to implement far-reaching social reform and improve the everyday life of their nations' citizens.

Tz'u-hsi was both. And then some.

Born in Peking (now Beijing), China, on November 29, 1835, Tz'u-hsi (pronounced "tsoo-shee") was chosen to enter the palace of Emperor Hsien-feng at age sixteen. Her role was that of a low-ranking concubine. However, her father had taught Tz'u-hsi to read and write, and she used those abilities to quickly rise to the envious position of emperor's secretary. In 1856, she was promoted to second-class imperial consort and gave birth to Hsien-feng's only heir, a son named Tsai-ch'un. Because the emperor's senior consort, Tz'uan, had failed to produce a male heir, five-year-old Tsai-ch'un became emperor when his father died in 1861. The young monarch was aided by a ruling council of eight elders.

Right in the middle of the decision making was his mother, Tz'u-hsi. She had become coregent with Tz'uan, but was more adept at political maneuvering, and had even greater influence because she was the young emperor's mother.

One of Tz'u-hsi's goals was to end the practice of foot binding. This Chinese custom, dating back at least to the year 960, called for the feet of young girls, five to twelve years old, to be tightly bound with linen to prevent them from growing. The big toe was bent back over the top of the foot while the other toes were curled underneath. The tiny, deformed foot of a young woman was considered a sign of beauty by Chinese men and gradually became a social requirement for marriage. Tz'u-hsi had long recognized the cruelty of the tradition, and spoke out for laws prohibiting it. The government finally banned the practice in 1912, after Tz'u-hsi's death.

Tz'u-hsi also fought to legalize marriage between citizens of Manchuria and those in the rest of China. Through her efforts and those of the ruling council, schools, foreign language centers, and railroads were built in various regions of China, along with a navy yard and arsenals based on the design of modern European facilities.

In 1872, the emperor married, ending the coregency of Tz'u-hsi. However, her separation from power proved to be short-lived, as did the emperor himself. He died in 1875, leaving a somewhat helpless widow to attempt to thwart the ambitions of her stronger and more intelligent mother-in-law. Somehow, Tz'u-hsi managed to reinstate herself into a position of high authority. She then adopted her four-year-old nephew, Kuang-hsu, and declared him the new emperor, grossly violating the strict laws of royal succession. She later convinced Kuang-hsu to marry her niece, further solidifying her influence on the throne.

During the late 1880s, Tz'u-hsi diverted money intended for the navy and used it instead to build herself a summer palace. When Japan and China went to war in Korea in 1894, the smaller but better-equipped Japanese forces easily defeated the larger Chinese navy. As a result, there was a widespread demand for reform in China. When he reached governing age, Kuang-hsu passed laws to end many of Tz'u-hsi's corrupt activities. Tz'u-hsi responded by having the emperor thrown into prison. She executed or exiled many of the reformers. She also had the emperor's favorite concubine drowned in a well.

In 1900, the Boxer Rebellion swept across China. Supported by Tz'u-hsi, peasants drove missionaries and other foreigners from China by burning their homes and churches. Many foreigners were killed, on order of Tz'u-hsi. In response, the armies of eight nations attacked Beijing and forced Tz'u-hsi into exile. She returned two years later after agreeing to peace terms.

Tz'u-hsi remained in power until her death in 1908. The day before she died, she appointed three-year-old P'u-i to succeed his uncle, Kuang-hsu. The emperor and his wife had died, suddenly and mysteriously. It is widely believed that Tz'u-hsi had them poisoned.

Queen Liliuokalani

The Last Queen of
Hawaii
1838–1917

The year was 1891, a time of unprecedented change in Hawaii. The population was growing by the day, but the number of native Hawaiians was in steady decline. Businessmen from the United States and Europe were every-where. And Queen Liliuokalani, destined to be the last monarch of Hawaii, took her place on the throne.

Liliuokalani Kamakeeha was born September 2, 1838, in Honolulu, Hawaii. As part of a Hawaiian tradition, she had been adopted as a baby by a local chief, Paki, and his wife, Konia. She had an older sister, Bernice, and two older brothers, James and David.

When Liliuokalani (lee-lee-ooh-oh-ka-la-nee) was four she was sent to the Royal School, run by missionaries from New England. They renamed her Lydia, the name she had received when she was baptized. Lydia didn't like the school but enjoyed learning English. It was an important skill, as the growing sugar industry was attracting an ever-larger number of Americans to the islands. Her greatest pleasure, however, was music, which she learned to read at a young age.

When Lydia was nine, her parents had a baby girl, who was immediately adopted by the king and queen. In December 1848, there was a measles epidemic and about 10 percent of the native population died. One of the victims was Lydia's baby sister.

The Europeans and Americans who were arriving in Hawaii in large numbers had brought the measles with them, along with a new set of priorities. Many of the newcomers saw the Hawaiian Islands in terms of business potential. Various farming techniques were being implemented. Whaling became a major industry. Sugar plantations and ranches were beginning to flourish. As the balance of the population shifted, so did the balance of power. The Americans and Europeans wanted to protect their own interests and saw the native government as irresponsible and insensitive to changing conditions. They acquired political positions and revised the constitution frequently, each time taking a little more power from the king. Land was being bought and sold at a rapid rate, usually by the haoles (outsiders).

Lydia married John Dominis, governor of the island of Oahu, on September 16, 1862. The wedding had been postponed two weeks after the sudden death of the four-year-old prince of Hawaii, heir to the throne. The boy's death was soon followed by the death of his father, King Kamehameha IV.

In 1863, King Kamehameha V named Dominis governor of Oahu. Talk of Hawaii becoming an American territory began to spread. Everywhere, decisions concerning the future of the islands were being made based on business considerations. Hawaiian culture and tradition was being washed away in a sea of dollars. In 1872, Kamehameha V died without an heir. For the first time in history, Hawaiians would elect their next king.

The two candidates were William Lunalilo and David Kalakaua, Lydia's brother. Lunalilo was elected, but within a year, died of tuberculosis. Another election was held, and again David was a candidate. This time he was elected, defeating Kamahameha's widow, Queen Emma. Kalakaua was forced to sign a new constitution in 1887, leaving the monarchy with little power. Hawaii was moving closer to democratic rule—but a democracy run by American businessmen, not native Hawaiians. Kalakaua left for the United States in 1890, desperately hoping to negotiate a trade agreement with Washington. In January 1891, he died in San Francisco. Before leaving, Kalakaua had appointed Liliuokalani to the position of regent. Now that the king had died, she was officially the queen of Hawaii.

Liliuokalani dismissed her brother's cabinet and chose her own. They were, again, all American businessmen who cared little about Hawaiian culture. But she secretly hoped for a return to the old ways, including a more powerful monarchy and a renewed emphasis on Hawaiian tradition. Then her husband died, leaving Liliuokalani alone against the men who were intent on overthrowing the monarchy. For the next two years, she worked hard to return to native Hawaiians many of the rights they had gradually lost. She sought a new constitution that would have strengthened the powers of the throne and limit the influence of anyone attempting to move Hawaii under the control of the United States.

Her efforts were in vain. On January 17, 1893, less than two years after Liliuokalani had become queen, armed Americans took over the government, and Hawaii was declared a republic. A revolt against the new government failed terribly, and Liliuokalani was arrested and held responsible. On January 24, 1895, she signed a statement, formally abdicating the throne. She had been told that by signing she might save the men charged in the revolt—and herself—from execution.

The former queen stood trial in the building that was once her palace. She was found guilty and sentenced to five years' hard labor. While in prison, she wrote many songs, including "Aloha Oe," which became famous around the world. Somehow, while she was losing everything else, Liliuokalani's love of music had endured. Eight months after her arrest, Liliuokalani and the other prisoners were released. In 1898, the Hawaiian Islands officially became a territory of the United States. After a visit to the United States, Liliuokalani returned to Hawaii, where she lived out her life in quiet, sad dignity. She died in Honolulu on November 11, 1917.

Aleksandra Kollontai

A Voice for
Russian Women
1872–1952

Aleksandra Kollontai was born into a world of comfort. As the daughter of a well-to-do Russian general, she had no need to ever see the side of life peopled by the disadvantaged and the poor. But her conscience forced her to take a hard look at the lives of her family's servants, and of peasant children she knew. What she saw moved her to action. And her actions helped change the lives of generations of men, women, and children all over the vast territory that would become the Soviet Union.

Aleksandra Mikhaylovna Kollontai was born on April 1, 1872, in St. Petersburg, Russia. She grew up in the lap of luxury, but by her teens had emotionally distanced herself from the trappings of wealth. At sixteen, she journeyed to Europe, touring the continent and exploring the writings of socialist and communist philosophers. (Socialism and communism are economic and political systems in which production of goods is controlled by the government and which seek to eliminate private ownership and competition.)

In 1893, Kollontai got married and had a son. Needing to see with her own eyes the problems of the working class, she and her husband visited a variety of factories. The more she saw, the more she became convinced that any government that would allow such suffering was the real cause of the problem. The only solution, she decided, was to overthrow the government. She began searching for groups of like-minded people who would be willing to do whatever it took to get rid of Russia's leader, the czar, and his repressive institutions.

Kollontai went to Switzerland to study economics. She believed that a thorough understanding of society's framework was necessary to reorganize it. Returning to St. Petersburg in 1898, she devoted herself full-time to the cause of revolution. Around 1905, she began to focus on the conditions and rights of women workers. She had developed the belief that women were entitled to equal pay for equal work, because the road to equality with men required financial independence from them. She also felt that women should be in charge of their own sexuality, as well as the timing and frequency of childbirth. Gradually, Kollontai concluded that women should be compensated by the state for their role in raising the next working generation. She called for government-funded child care and community facilities offering domestic services. As she saw it, women should be free to work without the burdens of child raising and household chores.

Aleksandra Kollontai poses with other attendees at the Second International Communist Woman's Conference in Moscow in 1921.

Kollontai fled to Europe in 1908 to escape arrest for her writings and activities. She criticized the "bourgeois" feminists for their refusal to participate in the workers' revolt. In 1915, she joined the Bolsheviks, a wing of the Russian Social Democratic party. When Vladimir Lenin led the Bolsheviks to power after the Russian Revolution of 1917, Kollontai was appointed a member of the party's Central Committee. She was the only woman selected.

In 1919, Kollontai established the Congress of Workers and Peasant Women. Her aim was to oversee the needs and rights of the women on whose backs the stumblings of the new government pressed most heavily. She was named the first director of the Women's Section of the Central Committee and used that position to attract more women into politics. As a direct result of her efforts, new laws were passed giving women equal rights concerning authority over children, division of property during divorce, control over earnings, and employment opportunities. It also established free hospital care for new mothers and their infants. (Halfway around the globe, women in the United States and Great Britain were making similar strides at the same time.)

Eventually, Kollontai saw that the communists cared more about the factories than about the people who worked in them. At the same time, many in the party grew tired of her preaching about women's sexual freedom. She was replaced.

In 1923, Kollontai became the first woman appointed as an ambassador. She served as Russian minister, first to Norway, then to Mexico, and finally to Sweden. These posts were, in part, the government's way of getting rid of her honorably. She continued to write and give speeches, but got much less attention. Kollontai died in Moscow on March 9, 1952.

Jeannette Rankin

First Woman in
the U.S. Congress
1880–1973

The date was April 2, 1917. The first woman ever elected to the United States Congress was about to begin her first day on the job. Such an event would have been dramatic on its own. But it was also the day President Woodrow Wilson asked Congress to declare war on Germany. That declaration could only come in a vote by the Senate and the House of Representatives. War had been raging all over Europe since 1914. It was the first major war of the industrial age, and sophisticated weapons such as submarines, antiaircraft guns, and chemical shells meant a level of destruction the world had never seen. For the first time in history, hundreds of thousands of soldiers were being killed and wounded, by both sides, in single battles. The only world power missing from the action was the United States. In winning election to Congress, Rankin entered what had always been a man's arena: national politics. Now she was about to tell the nation, and the world, what she thought of another favorite male pastime: war.

Rankin was born on June 11, 1880, in Missoula, Montana. After attending public schools in Missoula, she graduated from the University of Montana with a bachelor of science degree. She worked for a short time as a teacher and social worker, then discovered her calling while campaigning for woman's suffrage. Between 1912 and 1915, she lobbied in fifteen different states, helping women to gain the vote in Montana in 1914. Two years later, Rankin found herself facing a decision: continue the fight for national suffrage, or run for Congress from her home state.

Campaigning as a Republican in 1916, Rankin argued for the women's right to vote, prohibition, laws protecting children, and military preparedness for national defense. The following April, she was sworn in as the first woman ever to serve in Congress. For years, Rankin had fought against corruption in government, the lawlessness of the American West, and the suffering of the poor and mentally ill all over the country. She had worked tirelessly to improve conditions in factories, orphanages, and jails. And she had campaigned vigorously for woman's suffrage. The driving force behind all these efforts was her belief that people needed to work together, in peace, to solve problems.

On April 7, the House of Representatives would vote on whether the United States should enter the war. Any decision that would mean the loss of many thousands, perhaps millions, of lives would have been difficult. But Rankin's dilemma was even more complex. She knew that the first woman in Congress must not appear to be afraid of battle. Such a position would be

Jeannette Rankin makes her maiden address to Congress in 1917.

seen as weakness by many male voters and would surely hurt the chances for further gains by women in politics. Even the suffragettes, who had worked alongside Rankin, urged her to go along with her congressional colleagues and the president. Meanwhile, the pacifists, who had supported her antiwar philosophy, pleaded with Rankin to resist war.

The Senate had approved Wilson's declaration of war by a large margin, and now, at three in the morning, the House began its alphabetical roll call.

The gallery was filled to capacity, and as the votes were called out, those in favor of American involvement in the war were clearly in the majority. Then the clerk called for Jeannette Rankin's vote. Most everyone in Washington knew that Wilson's request for a declaration of war would be granted. The suspense lay in how the "lady from Montana" would vote. As Rankin rose, the chamber grew silent.

"I want to stand by my country," said Rankin. "But I cannot vote for war."

It is interesting to note, and often forgotten, that forty-eight other members of Congress also voted "no" that day. Rankin completed her term, often supporting legislation providing services for poor women and children. Because of redistricting she could not run for reelection. She probably would have been defeated anyway: as the war trudged on, a wave of patriotism rolled across the American landscape, and Montana voters tired of Rankin's pacifism. She lost a later race for the Senate, failing even to win the endorsement of the suffragists.

Rankin spent the next twenty years lobbying Congress for laws that would fight infant and maternal diseases, and as a field organizer for the National Council for the Prevention of War. In 1939, however, as the threat of world war returned, so did Rankin's political interest. Having suffered through the Great Depression, many Americans felt that the United States should take care of its own problems and not get involved in conflicts among other nations. This isolationist sentiment was especially popular in Montana, where Rankin easily defeated her Democratic opponent. In Congress, she consistently opposed President Franklin Roosevelt's plans for war. Again, she was not alone in her view that the United States should stay out of the conflict. But when the Japanese attacked Pearl Harbor, Rankin did stand alone. Roosevelt made his famous speech, describing December 7, 1941, as a "day that will live in infamy," and asked for a congressional declaration of war.

Jeannette Rankin cast the only opposing vote. This made her the only member of Congress to vote against U.S. involvement in both world wars. After her term was over, she continued to work for pacifism, the rights of women, and many civic causes.

In 1968, at age eighty-seven, Rankin spoke out against the Vietnam War. She led several thousand women in a protest at the Capitol in Washington, D.C. The success of the Jeannette Rankin Brigade led her to talk of another run for Congress, but a campaign never materialized. Rankin continued to travel, speak, and demonstrate right up until her death in Carmel, California, on May 18, 1973.

Eleanor Roosevelt

Expanding the
Role of First Lady
1884–1962

When Eleanor Roosevelt was eight years old, her mother died. Less than a year later, her younger brother died. Less than two years after that, her father died. Young Eleanor went to live at her grandmother's house, where she was tutored at home and had few friends. Yet this lonely girl would grow up to write books and magazine articles, give speeches to large audiences, meet with leaders of many nations, and donate her time to countless causes and organizations. She would also spend twelve years as the First Lady of the United States. In 1948, *Time* magazine called her "the best-known woman in the world."

Anna Eleanor Roosevelt was born on October 11, 1884, in New York City. Her parents were Elliott and Anna Hall Roosevelt, and she had two younger brothers. Elliott suffered from physical problems and alcoholism, and he was frequently in and out of sanitariums. Young Eleanor worshiped her father, despite his shortcomings. In 1892, her mother died of diphtheria. Eleanor's maternal grandmother had been designated legal guardian, and all three children went to stay with her. Eleanor studied French and music and volunteered with her family in helping the less fortunate members of New York society. All the while she dreamed of the day she would be reunited with her father. Later in 1892, Eleanor's brother Ellie, the middle child, contracted diphtheria and died. Then, in August 1894, her father died. Eleanor was not permitted to go to his funeral.

In 1899, Eleanor went to England to attend Allenswood, a girls' boarding school. The turn of the century gave Eleanor her first tastes of world events. In 1900, her Uncle Ted (Theodore Roosevelt) was elected president of the United States. The next year, she watched from her window as the funeral procession of Queen Victoria passed by in the streets below.

When Eleanor was eighteen she returned to the United States. She soon became reacquainted with Franklin Roosevelt, her fifth cousin and a student at Harvard University. They were married on March 17, 1905. That date had been selected because Uncle Ted would be in New York for the St. Patrick's Day parade. Twelve days before the wedding, Eleanor and Franklin had attended the president's second inauguration. They were sure it would be the only presidential inauguration they would ever witness.

Between 1905 and 1916, the Roosevelts had six children, one of whom died in infancy. By 1909, Eleanor and Franklin were commuting between their home in New York City and the family estate in Hyde Park, New York. In 1911, Franklin was elected to the state senate, and the Roosevelts moved to Albany.

Then, in 1913, he was appointed assistant secretary of the Navy, and Eleanor and Franklin were off to Washington. In 1920, Democratic presidential nominee James Cox chose Franklin to be his running mate.

After the Republicans won the 1920 election, Franklin returned to New York to practice law, and Eleanor joined the board of the League of Women Voters. Women had just won the right to vote, and Eleanor saw the organization as a way to remain politically involved—outside of her husband's career. She served on the legislative committee, reporting back to the members about any new laws Congress was considering. She was also instrumental in developing the league's policies.

During the summer of 1921, Franklin grew ill and seemed to be losing the use of his legs. He was soon diagnosed with infantile paralysis, or polio. His doctor suggested that Franklin might benefit from resuming some of his political activities, and urged Eleanor to help him. Although Eleanor was already active in the League of Women Voters and the Women's Trade Union League, she now pushed herself even harder, building on her own strengths as she helped Franklin increase his. She was soon serving as finance chairman of the Democratic State Committee. She wrote newspaper and magazine articles. She cofounded the Val-Kill Furniture Shop, a factory-store in Hyde Park that hired young farm workers who were unemployed in the winter. In 1926, she bought a private girls' school and taught sociology, government, and economics. And she worked as codirector of the Democratic Party's National Women's Committee—an extremely influential position. Meanwhile, Franklin regained his political ambition, if not his ability to walk, and in 1928 was elected governor of New York. Eleanor had mixed feelings about the election. While proud of her husband's accomplishment, and her own role in it, she was determined not to be pushed into the background to simply live the life of a governor's wife. She continued to teach, write, and lecture. She also

Eleanor Roosevelt addresses a crowd in New York City's Times Square. Roosevelt logged thousands of miles on the lecture circuit during her lifetime.

attended Democratic Party functions, and conducted inspections of hospitals and prisons.

In 1933, Franklin Roosevelt was elected president of the United States. Eleanor lived and worked in the White House for the next twelve years. She held the first press conference by a First Lady. She wrote a newspaper column, "My Day," which appeared in nearly two hundred newspapers six days a week. She traveled throughout the country, reporting back to Franklin on the concerns of Americans. She became a radio broadcaster, contributing her salary to charity. She gave lectures, spoke at colleges, and visited factories. She got involved in social relief programs, and talked about U.S. involvement in the war in Europe. She also traveled extensively abroad, most often to visit American servicemen.

President Roosevelt died on April 12, 1945. Eight months later, President Harry Truman appointed Eleanor to the U.S. delegation to the United Nations. As chair of the Commission on Human Rights, she helped draft the U.N. Declaration on Human Rights. She also remained active in party politics, especially during Adlai Stevenson's presidential campaigns in 1952 and 1956 and John F. Kennedy's campaign in 1960.

Eleanor Roosevelt maintained an active political and social life right up until death. She died in New York City on November 7, 1962.

Margaret Chase Smith

First Woman Elected to Both House and Senate
1897–1995

*M*argaret Chase Smith wasn't the first woman elected to the United States Senate. It only seemed that way. Perhaps that was because for nearly twenty-five years, she was the *only* woman seated in the upper chamber of Congress. Or perhaps it was because Smith, as a freshman senator, had stood alone on the Senate floor and rebuked Joe McCarthy's anti-communist tactics in what she called her "Declaration of Conscience." Or perhaps it was because she had a perfect attendance record in the Senate, answering every roll call during her tenure, even as she sought the

Republican nomination for president in 1964.

Margaret Madeline Chase was born in Skowhegan, Maine, on December 14, 1897. She was the first child born to Carrie and George Chase and was followed by three boys, then two girls. Her parents were poor and hardworking. What they lacked in formal education, they more than made up for in honesty and pride. The center of the universe, for Carrie, George, and their six children, was the family itself and the home they shared.

Margaret met her future husband while working as Skowhegan's telephone operator. Clyde Smith was a recently divorced town official, and he called her every night to ask the time. She was sixteen, he thirty-seven. Clyde was a born politician and in 1899 had become the youngest member of Maine's house of representatives. He served from 1915 until 1932. When she was seventeen, Margaret accepted a job as his part-time assistant. Fifteen years later, they were married. In 1936, Clyde was elected to the U.S. House of Representatives from Maine's Second Congressional District, and the Smiths went to Washington.

In April 1940, Clyde suffered a heart attack that left him too ill to carry out his responsibilities in Congress. He chose Margaret to succeed him in office. She agreed, reluctantly, and a few hours later he suffered a second heart attack and died. After his funeral, Margaret immediately returned to Congress and to the task of winning the next election. Clyde had entrusted her with his congressional seat. She refused to lose it, and she didn't. In December 1941, Smith provided a dramatic contrast to Jeannette Rankin, a representative from Montana. While Rankin cast the only vote opposing Roosevelt's request for a declaration of war, the "lady from Maine" had long been calling for strength through military preparedness.

Smith remained in the House until 1948, when one of Maine's senate seats opened up. In the race for her party's nomination, Smith collected more votes than her three male opponents combined. When she won the November election, the news vied for attention in the press with President Truman's upset victory. Smith had become the only woman ever elected to both the House and Senate.

As a freshman senator, Smith grew increasingly angered by Joseph McCarthy's uncontrolled and largely unsubstantiated accusations of communism against members of the State Department and other government agencies. In a speech delivered just a few yards from where McCarthy sat, Smith denounced the scare tactics and abuse of power and described the shame she felt as the result of his activities. "I am not proud," she said, "of the way we smear outsiders from the floor of the Senate and hide behind the cloak of congressional immunity." The public's response to the speech was almost unanimously positive. The press, in particular, seemed tickled by the fact that a woman (the *only* woman in the Senate), had put McCarthy and his comrades in their place. The immediate effect on McCarthy's quest was barely noticeable, but it set the stage for his ultimate downfall. Clearly, Smith had uttered what had been on the minds of millions of Americans. She went on to defeat McCarthy's handpicked opponent in the primary, then snared the election by skillfully using the new medium of television to get her message out.

In 1964, Smith announced her candidacy for president. True to her reputation for frugality, she spent very little on the campaign and was never considered a major candidate. Nevertheless, at the Republican convention, Smith's name was put into nomination by a senator from Vermont. There was not much chance of her winning, and Barry Goldwater got the nod as the party's candidate. But Smith gave millions of women, and thousands of Maine voters, a moment to remember as they watched the gray-haired senator receive twenty-seven votes on the first ballot.

Smith continued to serve in the Senate for eight more years. She was finally defeated in 1972, when her constituents decided it was time for new blood. Her retirement proved a difficult adjustment for Smith, and she distanced herself almost completely from the world of politics. On May 21, 1995, she suffered a stroke. She died eight days later.

Golda Meir

First Woman Prime
Minister of Israel
1898–1978

As a Jewish girl growing up in Russia and the United States, at the very beginning of the twentieth century, it would have been the wildest of fantasies for Golda Meir to imagine herself the prime minister of Israel. For one thing, it was a monumental task at that time—and would remain so for several decades—for a Jew just to survive. For another, the state of Israel would not exist until Golda was fifty years old. But by the time of her death, Meir had established a worldwide reputation. For many, she embodied the spirit that helped create the modern nation of Israel.

Goldie Mabovitch was born May 3, 1898, in Kiev, the capital of present-day Ukraine. She was the middle child of three girls born to Blume and Moshe Yitzhak Mabovitch. (Four boys all had died as very young children.) Most of Golda's earliest memories concerned hunger and terror. The family never had enough food to eat or money to pay the bills. Worst of all, they lived in constant fear of random mass violence, or pogroms, directed at Jews. In 1903, the family moved to Pinsk, about 250 miles (400 kilometers) to the northeast. But Golda's father had no intention of putting down roots there. His dream was to live in the *goldene medina,* the "land of gold," and he set off for New York City. Three years later, he sent for Blume and the three girls to come to Milwaukee, Wisconsin, where he had settled.

By the time Golda reached Milwaukee, she had grown aware of revolutionary groups who thought about, talked about, wished for, and planned to overthrow the Russian czar and his government. Mixed with these wild and dangerous schemes was another growing movement, called Zionism, which was concerned with reestablishing and resettling a Jewish homeland in Palestine, a bleak patch of land on the eastern shore of the Mediterranean Sea. Jews had been exiled from Palestine for nearly two thousand years, but over the centuries every generation carried on the dream of someday returning.

Life in America was not much easier than life in Kiev. Golda was forced to work in her mother's grocery store and frequently missed school. When she was fourteen, she left home to live with her older sister, Sheyna, in Denver. This proved to be a decisive turning point, for she remained in school and met the Zionists and Socialists with whom Sheyna had become associated. After graduating from Milwaukee Teacher's College, Golda obtained a job with the Labor Zionist party in 1917 and married Morris Meyerson. By that time, post-World War I agreements had resulted in Palestine's designation as the official Jewish homeland. The dream was beginning to approach reality.

Golda and Morris settled in Palestine. They lived on a collective farm, called a kibbutz, where each person did a share of the work and everyone was considered equal. In 1928, Golda became secretary of the Women's Labor Council of the Histadrut, a labor federation of Jewish workers. She was now a public figure, working to raise money to help found the state of Israel. The job required a great deal of travel, for the donations came from people and organizations in other countries. Like her father, Golda sacrificed time with her own family to work for a cause she believed in.

During World War II, Golda helped smuggle Jews who were fleeing Hitler's Nazi regime into Palestine. After the war, the United Nations assumed responsibility for the Jewish homeland issue. On May 14, 1948, Golda Meyerson was one of twenty-five people to sign Israel's Proclamation of Independence. Almost immediately, Egypt, Jordan, Syria, Lebanon, Iraq, and Saudi Arabia invaded the new nation. However, the attack failed, and Israel actually came away with more territory.

In 1949, Golda began a seven-year term as Israel's minister of labor. In 1956, Israeli prime minister David Ben-Gurion chose Golda as his foreign minister. At Ben-Gurion's request, the cabinet members began using their Hebrew names. Golda Meyerson, now separated from her husband, became Golda Meir.

Meir was named secretary general of the Israel Labor Party under Prime Minister Levi Eshkol. She became prime minister when Eshkol died in 1969. As head of a nation surrounded by hostile enemies, one of Meir's chief responsibilities was to build up Israel's military forces and establish and strengthen its alliances around the world.

On October 6, 1973, Egypt and Syria attacked Israel on Yom Kippur, the most solemn holiday of the Jewish calendar. The offensive caught Israel by surprise, and although the Israelis were able to drive out the invaders, their apparent lack of preparedness cost Meir her government. She stepped down in 1974. Meir spent the last four years of her life writing, speaking, meeting with world leaders, and working for Israel's peaceful coexistence with its Arab neighbors. She died on December 8, 1978, in Jerusalem.

Sirimavo Bandaranaike

First-Ever Woman
Prime Minister
1916–

In 1960, Sirimavo Bandaranaike assumed the leadership of Sri Lanka, becoming the world's first woman prime minister. It was a bittersweet victory, for her husband, the prime minister just a year earlier, had been removed from office by an assassin's bullet. Mrs. Bandaranaike held the post for five years, then was voted out. She returned to power in 1970, only to be defeated again at the polls seven years later. Many thought she was finished in politics. But with a little help from her daughter, she proved them wrong.

Sirimavo Ratwatte Dissawa was born on April 17, 1916, in Balongoda, Ceylon. Her father, Barnes Ratwatte Dissawa was descended from nobility. His ancestors had ruled the island until 1802, when it was conquered by the British. Her mother came from a wealthy family, as well, and Sirimavo, her two sisters, and four brothers lived a comfortable life in a mansion staffed by servants, cooks, and gardeners. Despite their affluence, the family was well liked by neighboring impoverished villagers.

At a young age, Sirimavo went to Ratnapura to attend the Ferguson Primary School. Next she journeyed to Colombo, the capital, to attend a Catholic convent school, where she learned English and studied literature. When she turned 24, her parents arranged for her to marry an aristocrat named Solomon West Ridgeway Dias Bandaranaike. A member of Parliament, Bandaranaike was a leader of the United Nationalist Party. His politics bordered on radical socialism, but he had nevertheless won the blessing of Sirimavo's father, and the marriage took place in 1940. They soon had three children, and Sirimavo devoted herself to raising them.

Meanwhile, Solomon worked to help Ceylon achieve independence. In 1947, those efforts proved successful, and Britain granted self-rule to the island nation. The following year, Solomon was elected to the House of Representatives and was also named minister of health and local government. He resigned in 1951 to form the Sri Lanka Freedom Party. When he was reelected to the House of Representatives, he formed an alliance among four parties and used that alliance's strength to win the office of prime minister in 1956.

As prime minister, Solomon wanted Ceylon to adopt a position of neutrality in world politics. He called for the removal of British military bases and established diplomatic relations with the region's most powerful nations, including China and the Soviet Union. He increased wages and enhanced workers' rights and pushed for the adoption of Sinhalese as the country's official language, replacing English, and wanted to make Buddhism the national religion. Some of these objectives, especially the last two, angered the Tamil Hindus, a powerful religious sect in Sri Lanka. Riots erupted and a state of emergency was declared. On September 25, 1959, the prime minister was assassinated by a Hindu monk.

The Sri Lanka Freedom party decided that Sirimavo was the best choice to lead the party and the nation. She worked to unite the various factions, and in July 1960, she was elected prime minister. The victory found Sirimavo caught between the tragic loss of her husband and the profoundly difficult challenges facing the island and its people. She immediately announced that she would follow the course charted by her husband. Sinhalese became the official language. She implemented a program to improve health services, housing, agriculture, and education. The government took control of the schools and newspapers, and large tracts of land, owned by the government, were made available for farming by peasants. Virtually every one of these programs made someone angry, and Sirimavo found herself constantly trying to appease one group or another. In 1965, with rising unemployment and cost of living and a shortage of consumer goods, Sirimavo's government was voted out.

In 1970, Sirimavo was again elected, but conditions had not improved and her government faced the same problems as before: widespread poverty, unemployment, shortages, and violence. In 1971, an opposition group tried to overthrow the Bandaranaike government. Before the fighting stopped, 1,200 people were dead and 16,000 had been arrested. The prime minister was widely criticized for the way she handled the emergency, and relations between Sirimavo and the people were strained for the next five years. She was repeatedly accused of corruption. During that time, Ceylon changed its name to Sri Lanka. In 1977, Sirimavo was again voted out of office. In 1980, she was found guilty of fraud, misuse of power, corruption, and nepotism. Stripped of her civil rights and banned from holding public office, Bandaranaike set out to clear her name and resume her political activities.

Just six years after being found guilty, Bandaranaike ran for president, but lost the election. Three years later, however, she won a seat in the National Assembly, where she headed the opposition. In November 1994, her daughter, Chandrika Bandaranaike Kumaratunga, was elected prime minister. Three months later, Kumaratunga was elected president. One of her first actions was to appoint her seventy-eight-year-old mother prime minister.

Indira Gandhi

First Woman Prime
Minister of India
1917–1984

*I*ndia and Pakistan went to war in 1971, the third such conflict between the two nations in just twenty-four years. But this time, India was led by Indira Gandhi, the country's first female prime minister. How would a woman handle the task? The question had been asked many times since 1966, when Gandhi had become prime minister. Could a woman, from a nation that had traditionally relegated females to the status of second-class citizens, lead a large male army to victory?

Indira was born in Allahabad, India, on November 19, 1917, the only child of Jawaharlal and Kamala Nehru. By the time she was twelve, Indira had organized the Monkey Brigade, a children's group that actively participated in India's fight for independence from Great Britain. Inspired by her parents' political activism—they were frequently imprisoned—and by the story of Joan of Arc, Indira grew increasingly involved in the independence movement. She, too, was to become intimately familiar with the inside of prison cells and the blunt pain inflicted by a policeman's club. She attended school in Switzerland and then studied at England's Oxford University, briefly, before returning to her homeland in 1941. While in London, Indira reestablished a relationship with a childhood friend from Allahabad, a journalist named Feroze Gandhi. They were married in March 1942, only to be arrested six months later for nationalist activities. Released from prison the following year, Indira and Feroze lived in Allahabad until 1946. By then, they had two sons, Rajiv and Sanjay.

In 1947, India gained its independence from Britain, and Jawaharlal Nehru became the country's first prime minister. His wife had died in 1936, and after the election Indira separated from her husband and went to live with her father, acting as his First Lady at important events. She attended coronations, funerals, speeches, and summit meetings with world leaders. In 1955, Gandhi became a member of the Indian National Congress, and four years later was elected president. Gandhi continued to work closely with her father until his death in 1964.

Nehru's successor, Lal Bahadur Shastri, chose Gandhi to be his minister of information and broadcasting. It was an important post, because India, a land of 500 million people, struggled under widespread illiteracy. Gandhi pushed for the manufacture of inexpensive radios, which could be purchased by large numbers of people. She increased broadcasting time and allowed television access to her opponents, as well as independent commentators. She also launched a radio program concerned with family planning.

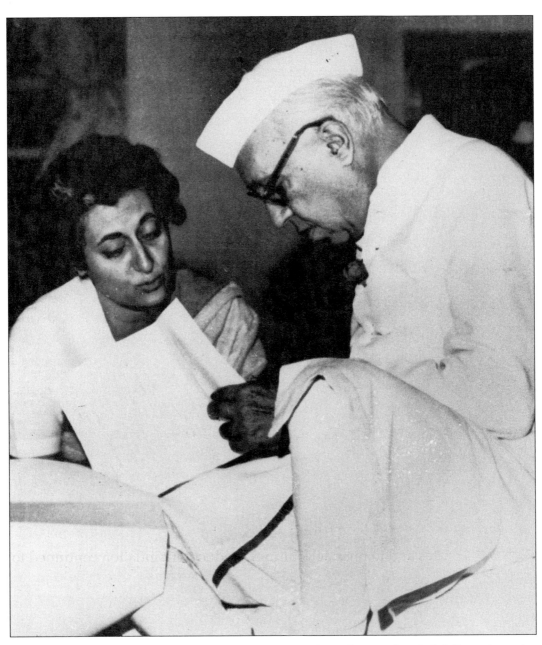

Indira Gandhi is shown here with her father, Jawaharlal Nehru, who served as India's first prime minister from 1947 to 1964. Gandhi took on the role of his "First Lady," because her mother had died in 1936.

When Prime Minister Shastri died suddenly in 1966, Gandhi was chosen as his successor. In 1967, she was reelected prime minister. Gandhi improved India's relations with the Soviet Union, giving her nation greater leverage and security in dealings with China, the powerful giant that shared India's northern border. She helped put the country's first satellite into orbit, further improving broadcast and communications services for the rapidly growing population. And she led the armed forces to a one-sided victory over Pakistan in 1971. In all phases of leadership, Gandhi seemed to exhibit vision and strength, and the people rewarded her the following year with an overwhelming electoral victory.

Gandhi's position was weakened, however, when political opponents accused her of violating election laws. When she began a voluntary sterilization program in an attempt to slow down population growth, many people believed she intended it to be mandatory, a suspicion that further eroded her popularity. In 1975, riots broke out. That same year, a high court ruled that Gandhi was guilty of 1971 election abuses, and she was told to give up her seat in Parliament. She responded by declaring a national state of emergency and imprisoning many of her opponents. These actions were widely considered to be unconstitutional. Gandhi was voted out of office in 1977.

Always prepared for another fight, Gandhi launched a comeback and won a landslide victory in the 1980 election. However, her final term in office was a troubled one. While she worked hard to improve India's relations with the United States and to raise agricultural productivity, inflation continued to soar and educational standards dropped sharply. Violence, so much a part of India's history, erupted again in several regions. Closer to home, Gandhi's son, Sanjay, was killed in an airplane crash.

In June 1984, Gandhi ordered a military invasion of the Golden Temple at Amritsar, the holiest of Sikh shrines as well as the headquarters for heavily armed Sikh extremists. The Sikhs, a militant religious group, had been committing acts of terrorism as part of their demands for greater political power. Four months later, on October 31, Gandhi was assassinated in New Delhi by two Sikh members of her own security force. The murder set off new rioting, and thousands of people were killed.

Gandhi was succeeded by her son, Rajiv, who served as prime minister until 1989, when he was removed from office under charges of corruption. In 1991, during an attempt to return to power, Rajiv, too, was assassinated.

Ella Grasso

First Woman Governor to Get There on Her Own 1919–1981

*E*lla Grasso will always be remembered as the first woman elected governor in the United States without following her husband into office. But a closer look reveals other accomplishments. She served as Connecticut's secretary of state, then landed a seat in the U.S. House of Representatives. Her election and reelection to the governorship were landslide victories. During her thirty years in politics, she never lost an election. Her popularity went beyond trust and respect. In an age of freshly acquired disillusionment about politicians in America, the people who voted for Ella Grasso—as well as many who didn't—loved her.

Ella Rosa Giovanna Tambussi was born in Windsor Locks, Connecticut, on May 10, 1919. Her parents, Giacomo and Maria, were Italian immigrants who had arrived in Windsor Locks seeking jobs. Maria worked for a time at a General Electric plant, but once Ella was born, stayed home to raise her. Around the same time, Giacomo left the factory where he had been working to open an Italian bakery. As more relatives from Italy arrived, and as the Tambussis made more friends, Ella's family began to extend well beyond their home. Before long, a close-knit community had developed in which Ella knew people wherever she went.

At home, Ella's mother made most of the major decisions. Like so many others, the Tambussis struggled through the Great Depression. But Giacomo had built a successful business, and their struggle was less severe than most. Meanwhile, Ella worked hard. She earned a scholarship to Chaffee, an exclusive private girls' school not far from Windsor Locks. There she got to know students from wealthy families from all over the country. She spent her days surrounded by the comforts of chauffeur-driven affluence, and her evenings back in the day-to-day routine of a working-class family in the middle of hard economic times. Ella walked with one foot in each world.

After achieving some financial security, the Tambussi family bought a small beach house in Old Lyme, on the Connecticut shore, and Ella enjoyed her summers there. In 1932, she met Thomas Grasso, a lifeguard from Hartford who was four years older but attracted by Ella's intelligence. They soon began dating.

In 1937, Ella received a scholarship to Mount Holyoke College. While there, she developed a keen interest in economics and the laws regarding labor and management. This interest eventually led her into politics. In 1940, Ella was active in the student organization supporting President Franklin Roosevelt's reelection. She agreed with Roosevelt's social welfare policies, especially his endorsement of laws promoting governmental responsibility toward labor. In 1940, she graduated Phi Beta Kappa from Holyoke with a bachelor's degree, went on to complete a master's in economics by 1942, and left school with a profound sense that her destiny lay somewhere in the field of public service.

Ella and Thomas were married in the summer of 1942. They moved into a house across the street from her parents. Tom worked as a teacher in East Hartford, while Ella took a job as the assistant director of research at the Connecticut War Manpower Commission. She was responsible for coordinating the state's defense-related industries. After the war, the agency was disbanded. Ella gave birth to a daughter in 1948. Three years later, a son arrived.

Throughout the early years of their marriage, Ella remained involved in labor and politics. She chaired the minimum wage boards for business, professional, and industrial workers. She was appointed to the state's Commission on Education. And she helped found the League of Women Voters in the town of Suffield. In 1951, Ella ran for one of the two general assembly seats in Windsor Locks. Her blend of liberal and conservative beliefs—she was a strong labor advocate but also looked for ways to cut government spending—appealed to a broad band of voters. She won the election.

Grasso rose quickly through the ranks of local politics and was widely considered a future star on the state level. In 1958, she became secretary of state, a post she held for twelve years. In 1970, she ran as a Democrat for the seat representing Connecticut's Sixth Congressional District. Appealing to voters in both worlds she had known at Chaffee, the wealthy and the working class, Grasso squeaked out a victory. She was reelected in 1972. But she soon tired of Washington and missed being with her family, so she set her sights on the statehouse.

Connecticut had a long history that included eighty-three governors, all men. As a candidate, Grasso went her own way. She refused to dress for the part or put on a show, choosing instead to remain "Mother Ella." In the end, that's what the voters wanted. They rewarded Grasso with a victory margin of more than two hundred thousand votes, an impressive showing in a state with fewer than three million people. Ella seemed to know most of them by name.

As governor, Grasso was immediately confronted with a shocking financial situation: a seventy million dollar debt. Further investigation put the figure at more than two hundred million. Grasso attacked the problem with common sense and frugality. The state sales tax was raised to 7 percent, the highest in the nation. Programs she had promised to fund were left dormant. The work week for state employees was increased, with no raise in pay. Grasso's popularity plummeted. The state slowly worked itself out of the financial deficit, and she was able to announce a budget surplus at the end of 1976. But it took the blizzard of 1978 to turn things around. Grasso's caring actions during that crisis convinced her constituents that she was still "Mother Ella." She won her reelection bid by 189,000 votes.

Then, in 1980, Grasso developed cancer. The disease proved extremely aggressive, and on December 4 she announced her resignation. Two months later, on February 5, 1981, Grasso died at Hartford Hospital.

Eugenia Charles

First Woman Prime
Minister in the Caribbean
1919–

*D*ominica is an island
nation of less than
three hundred square
miles and roughly eighty-three
thousand people, a population
about equal to that of Duluth,
Minnesota. Dominica is located
southeast of the U.S. Virgin
Islands and about three hundred miles from the coast of
Venezuela. Some people confuse it with the Dominican Republic, and most
would need some time to find it on a map. It certainly does not seem like the
kind of place that could ever produce a prime minister capable of standing on
the world stage for any length of time. At least it didn't until Eugenia Charles
came along.

Mary Eugenia Charles was born on May 15, 1919, in a town called Pointe Michel, not far from Dominica's capital city of Roseau. Her parents were John (J. B.) Baptiste and Josephine (Delauney) Charles. Eugenia's three brothers all became doctors and her sister became a nun. J. B., a former mason, made wise investments and established successful businesses, including his own bank. He died in 1982 at 107. Josephine, however, was the dominant figure in Eugenia's early years, as so much of family life in Dominica centers on mothers and grandmothers. Both parents emphasized the importance of education to all their children, but never tried to push them into any particular field.

Eugenia attended the Convent High School in Dominica, then St. Joseph's Convent on the island of Grenada, about two hundred miles (322 kilometers) south of her home. Having been urged by her father to learn shorthand while in school, Eugenia developed her skills by attending court proceedings and transcribing what she heard. This experience sparked an interest in the law. Eugenia attended the University of Toronto, where she received her bachelor's degree, and then went to England to advance her law studies at the London School of Economics and Political Science. (Dominica was, at that time, still a British colony.) By 1947, she had qualified to be a lawyer. Eugenia considered staying in England, but her parents persuaded her to return to Dominica. In 1949, she opened a practice in Roseau as the first woman lawyer on the island.

In 1967, Great Britain granted Dominica the right of self-rule. It was a major step toward complete independence. Meanwhile, with a successful legal practice established, Eugenia became increasingly interested in political issues. She began to write letters to the local newspaper, expressing her views on a variety of issues. The letters often were critical of specific government activities. In 1968, Prime Minister E. O. Le Blanc and his Labor Party passed a law that severely limited a citizen's right to express negative opinions about the government. The law aroused the anger of many people, including

Eugenia Charles, and a small group formed the Dominica Freedom Party. Although she took some convincing, Eugenia became the party's leader.

In 1975, Eugenia was elected to the house of assembly in the legislature, along with two other Freedom Party members. Eugenia became leader of the opposition, a post she would occupy for the next five years. On November 3, 1978, Dominica officially became an independent nation. Soon after, the island became the 151st member of the United Nations.

Eugenia often spoke out against Prime Minister Patrick John, whose government stood accused of an assortment of scandals. These included allegations that government officials were involved in drug trafficking and illegal dealings with South Africa. Moreover, inflation was on the rise, unemployment was out of control, and corruption was rampant. In May 1979, soldiers opened fire on a group of fifteen thousand demonstrators who were protesting recent government actions limiting freedom of the press and the rights of organized labor. A massive strike was staged, and the five largest trade unions called for the resignation of the prime minister. In June, the prime minister was forced from office, replaced by James Seraphine. Two months later, Hurricane David slammed into the island, killing forty-two people, leaving sixty-five thousand people homeless, and destroying the vital banana crop.

On July 21, 1980, the Dominica Freedom Party collected 52 percent of the vote, and Eugenia Charles became the new prime minister. She promised that her government would be "liberal, democratic, and anti-Communist," and immediately set out to rid Dominica of political corruption. Education, health care, and agriculture all benefited from Charles's reforms. Tourism increased and inflation was reduced dramatically. Then, in October 1983, the prime minister of nearby Grenada was overthrown. Believing that Cuba and the Soviet Union were behind the event, Charles asked U.S. president Ronald Reagan to send troops to restore law and order to Grenada. Two thousand soldiers from the United States and six Caribbean islands arrived within days, and the situation gradually returned to normal. The troops left Grenada in June 1985.

The Dominica Freedom Party won 59 percent of the vote in the July 1985 election. Eugenia Charles was again sworn in as prime minister, as well as minister of foreign affairs, finance, economic affairs, and defense. She remained prime minister until June 1995, when she was replaced by Edison James. During her fifteen years in office, Charles did much to improve the lives of the people of Dominica. And she created a unity among many of the island nations of the Caribbean.

Eva Perón

First Lady of Argentina
1919–1952

By the time Eva Perón's life ended after just thirty-three years, she had become one of Argentina's most popular and successful actresses. She had married one of the military's most powerful men and helped engineer his election to the presidency. She had amassed a personal fortune. And she had won the devotion of an entire nation. Perhaps most intriguing, much of her support came from the unsuccessful, the powerless, and the poor.

Maria Eva Duarte was born May 7, 1919, in a small town called Los Toldos. She was the youngest of five illegitimate children. Her mother was desperately poor and allowed her children to cook and clean for wealthy families in the area in return for food and money. As a teenager, Eva won a part in a school play and decided to make acting her career. She went to the capital city, Buenos Aires, where she eventually established herself as a motion picture and radio actress.

Eva found that she could use her physical appearance and her modest fame to gain access to influential men. The most powerful of these was Colonel Juan Perón, who was part of a military group that had taken over the government in 1943. He had been named secretary of labor and social welfare. In 1944, President Edelmiro Farrell named Perón both vice president and war minister. That same year, Eva became Perón's mistress. They were married in 1945.

Their relationship provided a tremendous boost to the careers of both Eva and Juan Perón. The actress was now earning a great deal of money, and even though the colonel had been removed from power by a military takeover in 1945, this would prove to be a temporary setback. Eva, driven to success by her impoverished childhood, believed strongly in her husband's ability to lead—and in her own ability to help him by inspiring the nation's poor. The Peróns traveled all over Argentina, instilling in the people a vision of how much better their lives could be. Calling for minimum wages, better working conditions, and more opportunity, the couple generated a huge base of support, especially among the *descamisados* (the shirtless ones) and the labor unions. That support carried Juan Perón to the presidency in 1946.

Once in office, he turned the management of organized labor over to his wife, who had charmed union crowds with her beauty, spirit, and speaking ability. Eva quickly got rid of any leaders who did not solidly support her husband. Meanwhile, her frequent trips to the slums and her gifts of food and money to the poor raised her popularity to a level never before

This stamp, issued in 1952 in commemoration of Eva Perón, demonstrates her importance to the people of Argentina.

known by a political figure in Argentina. When a charitable organization, the *Sociedad de Beneficiencia,* refused to make her its honorary chairman, she disbanded it and formed the Maria Eva Duarte de Perón Social Welfare Foundation. Its activity, under her absolute control, was the boat she rode on a seemingly endless sea of power.

That power was either unseen or ignored by the masses. Behind the scenes, Eva and Juan Perón had created a stronghold over virtually every operation of government and industry. Opponents were repressed, critics were quieted, and information that flowed through radio and television was carefully censored. The world's postwar demand for beef and wheat fueled Argentina's economy, and there was plenty of money for social programs. Some of that money ended up in the Peróns' personal bank account, but a good deal of it went toward fulfilling the president's promises for reform. Working conditions were improved, wages were raised, and educational standards were enhanced. Eva, working as unofficial minister of health and labor, raised money to build hospitals, schools, homes for the elderly, havens for unwed mothers, and orphanages. Her programs provided food and clothing for the poor, and a feeling of security for millions.

Eva also worked hard for feminist causes. She campaigned for women's voting rights, equal opportunity and pay, and social equality. A law passed in 1947 gave women the right to vote and run for office at the national level. Eva herself ran for vice president in 1951. Although her popularity was at an all-time high, the military blocked her efforts, and she did not succeed. A short time later, she suffered an emotional collapse. She developed cancer and died on July 26, 1952.

Without the chief source of his own popularity, Juan Perón was removed from power in 1955. He returned to the presidency in 1973 and remained in office until his death the following year. Ironically, Juan Perón's third wife, Isabel, had run successfully as his vice presidential candidate. She succeeded him as president after he died.

Isabel, then, was just one of the women who enjoyed the benefits of Eva Perón's efforts. Eva (or Evita, as she is still known to the world) had worked tirelessly to change the lives of so many in Argentina. She certainly accomplished much in her thirty-three short years.

Bella Abzug

A Fighter All the Way
1920–1998

Bella Abzug was a congresswoman from New York. She wasn't the first woman to serve in the United States Congress. She wasn't even the second or the third. But she was, in many ways, the best known. She became a national figure, bigger somehow, than the office she held. And she changed politics for women. As Geraldine Ferraro, the first woman ever to run for vice president of the United States said, "If it weren't for Bella, there'd be no Gerry."

Bella Savitzky was born in New York City on July 24, 1920, the same year, she would later tell many people, that women finally got the right to vote. She was the second daughter of Esther and Emanuel Savitzky, both children of Jewish refugees from Russia. From them Bella learned to appreciate what she had, even as she was striving for something better. By age seven, she could recite many of the Hebrew prayers she had heard in synagogue. She was the fund-raising leader of the Jewish Community Center Youth Group, yelling her speech to passengers getting off trains as her companions collected pennies for Palestine. She was a superb athlete, a good student, and as outspoken as any kid in the East Bronx.

As Bella approached high school age, her grandfather and her father died within a short time. In 1938, she graduated from Walton High School and set her sights on becoming a lawyer. Bella enrolled in Hunter College's new campus in midtown Manhattan. Within weeks she'd been elected freshman class president, and within two years was president of the entire student body of four thousand women. But Bella's political interests stretched beyond the confines of Hunter. She believed strongly that the United States should act to stop Adolf Hitler and the spread of Nazism. She knitted countless wool hats for the troops and listened anxiously to the latest war bulletins several times a day. An urge to help the world was brewing inside her.

After graduation, Bella applied to Harvard Law School but was turned down because of her sex. Outraged at the injustice, she went to Columbia. During the summer, while vacationing in Miami, she met Martin Abzug, who worked for his father manufacturing blouses. He had just been drafted, and they spent the next couple of years writing letters and seeing each other whenever they could. On June 4, 1944, Bella and Martin got married.

After graduating from Columbia, Bella passed the New York State bar and landed a job at a law firm. In 1948 the couple had a baby girl, and named her Eve. Soon after, Bella opened her own law office and began defending clients caught up in the McCarthy communism hysteria. (Judges and other lawyers, unaccustomed to female attorneys, often mistook Bella for a secretary. It was then that she began wearing large hats to help make herself more recognizable.) In 1952, Bella gave birth to a second girl, Liz, and the family moved to suburban Mount Vernon. Martin was working on Wall Street.

In the early 1960s, Bella got involved with a women's group protesting nuclear weapons and finally felt she was doing something to save the world. In 1965, the family moved to Greenwich Village in lower Manhattan. By 1967, Bella had become one of the leaders in the peace movement against nuclear arms and the war in Vietnam. Then Richard Nixon, a man Bella detested, was elected president. She decided to run for Congress.

Bella's opponent in the primary was seeking his eighth term in office. The experts told her she was crazy, but Bella pulled off the upset. Her gift of gab, raspy voice, and sense of humor—and her passion for the issues—made her the favorite to win the election against radio personality Barry Farber. She constantly spread her message: it was time to get rid of the callous politicians and elect representatives who knew and cared about the citizens of the district. People listened. Bella won by almost ten thousand votes.

In Congress, Bella was outspoken and ignored some of the traditional House rules. At a reception for freshman congressmen, she told President Nixon he was doing a lousy job of getting America out of Vietnam. She continued to work for an end to the war, and for greater opportunity for women in politics. Behind the scenes, her loud voice and trademark hats angered the old-guard politicians. In 1972, it was announced that, because of dwindling population, Manhattan's four districts would be reduced to three. Bella's district was gone.

Rather than leave quietly, Bella decided to fight back. She challenged William Ryan for his seat in the House. Ryan had been very ill for some time, and Bella's aggressiveness further aroused her critics and the public. When she lost to Ryan in the primary, she promised to support him. Then on September 17, Bill Ryan died, and the Democrats needed a candidate. They chose Bella. She had four opponents, including Bill Ryan's widow, Priscilla. Bella got more votes than the other four candidates combined.

Bella raged through her second term, putting in fourteen-hour days, screaming for ways to shake up the system, and rooting for Nixon's downfall. She coauthored the Freedom of Information and Privacy Acts and was one of the first members of Congress to vote for the Equal Rights Amendment. She also helped found the National Women's Political Caucus.

Bella won a third term in 1974, but declined to run in 1976. She took aim at the Senate, instead, but failed to win the nomination. The following year, she lost her bid for the New York City mayor's office and announced that it would be her last campaign.

In 1991, Bella presided over the Women's Congress for a Healthy Planet. She also continued to write and lecture and worked to increase the number of women in elected office. She was founder and cochair of the Women's Environmental Development Organization (WEDO). Bella died March 31, 1998, after heart surgery.

Shirley Chisholm

First African-American
to Run for President
1924–

$\int$ hirley Chisholm was
the first African-American
woman to be elected to
the United States Congress.
While many people might have
been content with such a dis-
tinction, Chisholm had her
sights set on an even loftier goal:
the presidency.

Shirley Anita St. Hill was
born in Brooklyn, New York, on November 30, 1924, in the very district she
would later represent. Her parents were Charles and Ruby (Seale) St. Hill.
Her father grew up in Guyana and worked as an unskilled laborer in a burlap
bag factory. Ruby was from Barbados and worked as a seamstress. In order to
save money for their children's education, Charles and Ruby sent Shirley and

her three younger sisters to live with their maternal grandmother on a Barbados farm. They returned to Brooklyn in 1935 with a British elementary school education and distinctive Barbados accents.

Shirley graduated from Girls High School in 1942. Four years later, she received her bachelor's degree in sociology from Brooklyn College. She had become interested in school politics and was active in the campaigns of several fellow classmates. She had also won numerous prizes for her debating skills and graduated cum laude. Three years after college, Shirley married Conrad Chisholm. In 1952, she earned her master's degree in education at Columbia University. A year later, she became director of a child-care center, as well as a consultant to the New York City Bureau of Child Welfare. She was a member of the board of directors at the Brooklyn Home for Aged Colored People. And she was active in the NAACP (National Association for the Advancement of Colored People), the Democratic Women's Workshop, the League of Women Voters, and the Bedford-Stuyvesant Political League. She became increasingly angered by the injustices faced by women, children, and African-Americans. Her deep involvement in her community rekindled her interest in politics, and she built a solid foundation of trust and support among the voters. In 1964, at the urging of many residents of her predominantly African-American and Puerto Rican district, Chisholm ran for a seat in the state legislature. She became only the second African-American woman elected to the New York state assembly. While in office, she was a strong advocate for child welfare and the creation of day-care centers.

In 1968, Chisholm decided to run for the United States House of Representatives from New York's Twelfth Congressional District, which is located in a poor Brooklyn neighborhood called Bedford-Stuyvesant. Running under the slogan "Unbought and Unbossed," she won the November election by fewer than eight hundred votes. She then headed for

Washington, where she continued to work for minority and women's rights, sticking closely to the issues that most affected her urban constituents.

Four years later, Chisholm surprised everyone by announcing her candidacy for president. She was the first minority person ever to do so. She did not really expect to win the election, or even the nomination. Her goal, as she explained it to an audience in a Brooklyn Baptist church, was "to repudiate the ridiculous notion that the American people will not vote for a qualified candidate simply because he is not white or because she is not male." Chisholm's campaign was somewhat disorganized and underfunded and did not use the media well. The result was very little exposure for the candidate. However, Chisholm did capture 10 percent of the votes at the Democratic National Convention, a very respectable showing.

Shirley Chisholm served in the House of Representatives for seven terms. While in office, she created the National Political Congress of Black Women, called for the end to British arms sales to South Africa, and proposed funding increases to extend the hours of child-care facilities. She was also an early advocate of legalized abortion and a strong supporter of gay and lesbian rights. Increasingly, she found herself working hard just to help women, children, and minorities avoid losing the gains they had made over the previous decade. Chisholm grew frustrated at operating in an ever-more-conservative political climate. She retired from Congress in 1983 to pursue a teaching career at Mount Holyoke College. However, she never stopped encouraging women to "move into politics on a leadership level." Shirley Chisholm had cleared a path behind her, and scores of women would follow in her footsteps.

Margaret Thatcher

Solid Leadership in
Shaky Times
1925–

*M*argaret Thatcher assumed the office of prime minister of Great Britain in 1979. In the process, she became the first woman to hold such a position of power since that country's parliamentary form of govern ment had emerged in the thir- teenth century. By the time she left office in 1990, Thatcher had served longer than any British prime minister in 150 years.

Born in Grantham, England, on October 13, 1925, Margaret was the daugh- ter of Alfred and Beatrice Roberts. Her mother was a dressmaker, her father a grocer. Margaret attended Oxford University, where she received her bachelor of science degree in chemistry. At Oxford, she was elected president of the university's Conservative Association. After graduating, she worked as a research chemist and went to law school. Her interests and talents were numerous, but the dream of a political career had burned in her heart at least since 1943, when her father was elected mayor of Grantham.

In 1950, Margaret became the youngest person ever to run for Parliament. She was unsuccessful and lost again the following year. In 1951, Margaret married Denis Thatcher. She began her law practice in 1953, and five years later she was elected as a Conservative (or Tory) to Parliament's House of Commons for the North London district of Finchley. She held the seat until 1992.

Thatcher achieved another first in 1970 when she was appointed secretary of state for education and science. She was the first and only woman chosen to serve in Prime Minister Edward Heath's cabinet. When Heath resigned in 1974, Thatcher took his place as Tory party leader. Five years later, she led the Conservatives to a majority in the House of Commons and was named prime minister.

As a cabinet member, Thatcher had believed her party had been drifting toward the center of the political spectrum and worked to move it in a more conservative direction. As prime minister, she attempted to fight inflation through reduced spending, except in the areas of defense and law enforcement. She lowered income taxes and opposed welfare, as part of a free enterprise platform. She turned many government industries over to private business. And she tightened restrictions on immigration.

The immediate results were not positive. The economy produced less, so fewer workers were needed. More than a million people lost their jobs in one year as unemployment doubled from 1980 to 1981. In the inner cities all over Britain, random violence turned into widespread rioting. Thatcher refused to back down on her policies, believing they would eventually produce beneficial results. But public approval had dwindled, and both Thatcher and her party were in serious danger of being replaced in a new election. The prime minister needed to show her strength and leadership qualities. Her opportunity arrived in June 1982, some eight thousand miles (12,800 kilometers) away, in the Falkland Islands.

The Falklands are located in the South Atlantic, four hundred miles (640 kilometers) off the coast of Argentina. Britain had occupied the islands since 1833, but for a century and a half, Argentina continued to claim the Falklands as its own. Then, on April 2, 1982, Argentine troops seized the islands. Negotiations regarding the status of the islands, which had been going on since 1966, halted abruptly, and Thatcher sent navy warships on a journey to recapture British territory. As the world watched, British ships sped across the Atlantic and the equator toward the Falklands. Meanwhile, Argentine troops prepared for battle. That battle took place during the last half of May and the first half of June. By the time Argentina surrendered on June 14, about two hundred fifty British troops and more than seven hundred Argentine soldiers had been killed.

Sensing an upturn in her popularity, Thatcher called for an election in 1983. The Conservatives won by a large majority. Thatcher used her second term to continue her programs, and unemployment finally began to drop and inflation slowed. She broke a bitter strike by the miners, which had dragged on for more than a year. And she resolidifed ties with the United States through a strong relationship with President Ronald Reagan.

When Thatcher won a third term in 1987, she decided to really get serious about her reform programs. She privatized the water and electric utilities and deregulated radio and television. Then, in 1990, a "poll tax" designed to help support local government was levied on British citizens, sparking demonstrations and rioting. Further cuts in the income tax helped cause a rise in

In this 1985 photo, then-Prime Minister Margaret Thatcher says good-bye to then-U.S. President Ronald Reagan after Thatcher addressed a joint meeting of Congress. Thatcher and Reagan embodied the strongly conservative political and economic mood of the 1980s.

inflation and interest rates. Thatcher then angered members of her own party when she refused to support Britain's participation in the European Monetary System, a plan to introduce a common currency for all member nations. When her leadership was again challenged in 1990, Thatcher realized her support had declined sharply, and she resigned.

Although Margaret Thatcher has been out of office for many years, the word *Thatcherism* is still used to describe leadership that holds fast to its beliefs despite strong public opposition. Margaret Thatcher embodied that kind of leadership. Her central values were hard work, thrift, and responsibility. She was certain those values were right for British citizens and the British nation. Her vision of a greater Britain prevented her from caving in to the pressures of advisers and the general public. She pressed on, sure that what she was doing was right. And while her failures were many, Margaret Thatcher succeeded in redefining what a strong leader—and a very shrewd politician—could accomplish.

Jeane Kirkpatrick

First Woman U.S.
Ambassador to the
United Nations
1926–

When Jeane Kirk-patrick was teaching political science at Georgetown University in the 1970s, she didn't expect her own influence to reach much beyond a good lecture. But by 1981, she had been chosen by President Ronald Reagan to be U.S. ambassador to the United Nations. And by 1987, she herself was considered a prospective presidential candidate by many political experts.

Jeane Duane Jordan was born on November 19, 1926, in Duncan, Oklahoma. Her father, Welcher, drilled oil wells. Her mother, Leona, spent a good deal of time instilling in Jeane a love of reading and writing. Jeane's brother was born when she was eight, and six years later the family moved to Mount Vernon, Illinois. There, Jeane's love for literature and classical music emerged. An excellent student, she edited her school newspaper and landed roles in several plays. She also developed a powerful interest in history and politics and was deeply affected by the 1941 attack on Pearl Harbor by Japanese bombers. In 1944, Jeane enrolled in Stephens College in Columbia, Missouri. After completing the two-year program, she was accepted at Barnard College in New York City. She chose political science as her major. Around the same time, the recently formed United Nations was settling into its new headquarters on the east side of Manhattan.

After her first year at Barnard, Jeane spent the summer in Montreal, working hard to master the French language. In 1948, she received her bachelor of arts degree. That September, seeking an advanced degree in political science, Jeane enrolled in a postgraduate program at Columbia University. By the time she completed her master's degree requirements, Jeane was just one seminar and a dissertation short of a doctoral degree. However, her father insisted she get a job and earn some money, so she headed for Washington, D.C.

Armed with letters of recommendation from Columbia, Jeane landed a job in the office of Evron Kirkpatrick, a high-ranking State Department official. Kirkpatrick had taught Hubert Humphrey at the University of Minnesota and helped him get elected mayor of Minneapolis. By the time Jeane arrived in Washington, Humphrey was a Minnesota senator.

In 1952, Jeane won a fellowship to study at the Institute de Science Politique at the University of Paris. She sailed for France in September. The following year, Jeane was back in Washington. She landed a position as a research associate at George Washington University. Her first assignment was to interview Chinese prisoners of war who had been captured in

During her tenure as U.S. ambassador to the United Nations, Jeane Kirkpatrick was a vocal proponent of a strong military and had a major impact on U.S. foreign policy.

Korea. The soldiers were asking not to be sent back to China, and Jeane's job was to find out why. What she learned about the tactics of a totalitarian government shocked her and would alter her beliefs forever.

Meanwhile, Jeane and Evron were seeing each other socially. They got married on February 20, 1955. The couple honeymooned at a political science convention in Chicago. Their first child was born in July 1956. They would have two more sons, with Jeane at home as a full-time mother and part-time research associate at Amherst College. Both Jeane and Evron were interested in—and concerned about—communism and its accompanying aggression and persecution.

When Lyndon Johnson won the nomination for president in 1964, he chose Hubert Humphrey as his vice presidential running mate. The Kirkpatricks attended the Democratic National Convention and worked together on Humphrey's speeches. In 1967, Jeane became an associate professor of political science at Georgetown University.

By 1979, Jeane Kirkpatrick was a well-known writer and scholar. That year she published a magazine article criticizing President Jimmy Carter's approach to foreign policy and human rights. In the article, she described the difference between communist dictatorships and authoritarian regimes and asserted that right-wing authoritarian governments deserved the support of the United States. Soon after, Ronald Reagan invited her to join his campaign. Her ideas on human rights formed the basis of Reagan policy in that area. A few months later, he asked her to be the United States ambassador to the United Nations. She was the first woman ever to hold that post, serving from 1981 until 1985.

As U.N. ambassador, Kirkpatrick oversaw a staff of 130 people, consulted with the president, and worked with members of his cabinet. She met with world leaders and was instrumental in helping shape U.S. foreign policy during the early 1980s. Kirkpatrick was extremely influential in the nation's involvement with the Nicaraguan government, advocating military aid to the rebels trying to overthrow the communist regime, a position President Reagan supported. She also helped negotiate a peaceful resolution to a potentially disastrous situation between Israel and Iraq.

Kirkpatrick resigned her post at the United Nations in 1985, having served longer than any U.S. ambassador since the 1950s. After her resignation, she immediately left the Democratic Party and became a registered Republican. She continues to write books, lecture, and teach. She also serves on several governmental advisory boards and is widely considered a leading expert on foreign affairs.

Violeta Barrios de Chamorro

First Woman President
in Central America
1930–

*N*icaragua in 1990 was a poor, war-torn nation. Civil war had been raging for eight years. Soldiers obligated to fight for the government and rebels determined to overthrow that government were killing each other on a daily basis. Assassinations were frequent, and democracy was nowhere in sight. Then along came Violeta Chamorro, a woman with almost no political experience, in a country where no woman had ever been president. The odds were not favorable. Yet not only was she elected, but she held onto the presidency for seven years.

Violeta Barrios was born on October 18, 1930, in Rivas, Nicaragua. She was one of seven children. Her parents were wealthy landowners, and Violeta spent a happy childhood enjoying the many outdoor activities available on a cattle ranch. Her parents knew well the value of a good education—for their sons and daughters—and insisted that Violeta attend women's schools in the United States. She enrolled in Our Lady of the Lake Catholic School for Girls in San Antonio, Texas. After graduating, she went on to Blackstone College in Virginia but returned to Nicaragua when her father died in 1948.

In 1950, Violeta met Pedro Joaquín Chamorro Cardenal. Pedro's family was also quite wealthy and had been active in politics for many years. They published a controversial newspaper called *La Prensa,* which criticized the Somoza family, a series of dictators who had been running Nicaragua since the mid-1930s. In the early 1940s, Pedro and his parents were exiled. They returned to Nicaragua in 1948 and resumed publishing their newspaper.

Violeta and Pedro were married within a few months of their meeting. They had five children, although only four survived. Pedro spent much of the next twenty-five years speaking out against the activities of Anastasio Somoza García, his son, Luis Somoza Debayle, and Luis's brother, Anastasio Somoza Debayle. The Somozas had eliminated most of their political opponents, altered the constitution to favor themselves and their friends, rigged elections, and used the powerful National Guard to enforce their will. The family dictatorship was eventually brought down by a long series of corrupt activities, capped by the 1978 assassination of Pedro Chamorro. The 1972 earthquake in the capital city of Managua had devastated the nation. Nicaraguans from all parts of society were tired of the political strongmen, and peasant guerrillas joined forces with students and revolutionaries from all walks of life. Violeta Chamorro, who had taken over publication of *La*

Prensa after her husband's death, supported the Sandinista National Liberation Front (FSLN). In 1979, the FSLN overthrew the Somoza government, and Daniel Ortega Saavedra came to power.

Ortega had preached the need for democracy in Nicaragua. But soon after taking over the government, he seemed to change his position, imposing major reforms on Nicaraguan society. Some of those reforms would benefit the nation. The Sandinistas worked to improve literacy, for example, as well as health care. But perhaps the aggressive manner in which the government acted offended and frightened the people, who had just ended forty years of dictatorship. What was left of Somoza's army, now known as the Contras, had reorganized near the Honduran border. Attacks by the Contras, aided by the U.S. Central Intelligence Agency, flared up. Thousands died, and perhaps hundreds of thousands became refugees.

Among the many voices protesting, Violeta Chamorro's was one of the loudest. She rallied the people, urging them to follow the tide of self-rule that was rising everywhere. "All across the world," she said, "people are burying communism and proclaiming democracy." Chamorro was chosen as the candidate of the National Opposition Union.

By 1989, Ortega had agreed to hold free elections. On February 25, 1990, Nicaragua held elections for the first time in 170 years. Violeta Chamorro defeated Ortega, becoming the first woman president ever in Central America. Ironically, her own four children were split in their political beliefs: two supported the Sandinista government, and two opposed it. The new president faced the task of restoring peace in her own home, and in the nation.

Chamorro moved quickly to end the draft and reduce the size of the army and worked to restore private property rights. She struggled with widespread unemployment and a growing national debt. But her aim was toward healing. She ended the civil war and granted amnesty to political prisoners. She also allowed several Sandinistas to keep their positions in the military. Most notably, Humberto Ortega, Daniel's brother, stayed on as chief of the armed forces. Perhaps most remarkable, Chamorro restored peace to an economically bankrupt country without the aid of any major foreign political power. The fighting has almost completely stopped, and Nicaragua is, at last, a democracy. Chamorro left office in 1997.

Sandra Day O'Connor

First Woman
Supreme Court Justice
1930–

A little girl grew up on a huge, dusty ranch in southeastern Arizona during the 1930s. There were no other children around, so the girl made friends with raccoons, goats, bobcats, crows, turtles, and porcupines. By the time she was ten, she could ride a horse, brand cattle, operate a tractor, and shoot a rifle. She could do just about anything a boy could do. Meanwhile, a few thousand miles away, a huge white building with tall pillars stood in the nation's capital. Nine people dressed in black robes worked in that building. They were judges in the Supreme Court. They had always been men.

Sandra Day was born on March 26, 1930, in El Paso, Texas. She was the oldest of Harry and Ada Mae Day's three children. Though born in Texas, Sandra grew up on the Arizona ranch that had been in the family since her grandfather, Henry Day, bought three hundred square miles of land from the federal government in 1880. Sandra's home had no electricity or running water. Her mother cooked meals on a wood-burning stove and kept food cold with a block of ice. She stayed current on world events by subscribing to newspapers and magazines. The house was always filled with books, and Sandra became an avid reader.

When Sandra was five, she went to live with her maternal grandmother in El Paso. Her parents believed their daughter was too bright for the local school in Arizona. They wanted her to get a good education, so she was enrolled in Radford, a private girls' school in El Paso. She graduated from Austin High School when she was sixteen. The family traveled a great deal to all parts of the United States, as well as Cuba, Mexico, and Honduras. After several trips to California, Sandra decided to attend Stanford University. There she majored in economics and graduated magna cum laude with a bachelor's degree in 1950. Two years later, she received her doctor of law degree, graduating third in her class. While working on the editorial board of the *Stanford Law Review,* Sandra met John Jay O'Connor, a fellow law student one year behind her. They were married in 1952. After graduating, Sandra interviewed with numerous law firms in Los Angeles and San Francisco, but none would consider hiring a female lawyer.

The O'Connors lived in West Germany for three years while John fulfilled his obligations to the military. Sandra worked there as a lawyer. By the time their first son was born in 1957, Sandra and John were back in Arizona, living near Phoenix. Two years later, Sandra started her own law practice. She also became involved in various local organizations. She served as a member of the Maricopa County Board of Adjustments and Appeals and the

Governor's Committee on Marriage and Family. And she was the Republican Party's district chairman from 1962 to 1965.

In 1965, Sandra became assistant attorney general for Arizona. When a state senator gave up her seat in 1969, Sandra was chosen by Governor Jack Williams to replace her. The following year, Sandra won the seat in the general election and was reelected in 1972. That same year she was named majority leader, the first woman ever to hold that office in any state legislature in the country. During her five years in the Arizona senate, O'Connor supported programs to limit government spending, and to improve working conditions and compensation for women. She voted for the Equal Rights Amendment (ERA) and to restore the death penalty in Arizona.

At the end of her second full term in the legislature, O'Connor decided to switch branches of government. In 1974, she was elected as a judge to the Maricopa County Superior Court. On the bench, O'Connor was known as strict but fair. She ordered the death penalty in at least one case. At the same time, she expressed concern over prison conditions in her state. In 1979, she was chosen by Governor Bruce Babbitt for the Arizona Court of Appeals. Meanwhile, Ronald Reagan was campaigning for the presidency. Reagan had angered women by opposing the ERA, but then he promised that if elected he would appoint at least one woman to the Supreme Court. In June 1981, Associate Justice Potter Stewart retired and the search was on for a replacement. On July 7 President Reagan announced his nomination of Sandra Day O'Connor as the first woman on the Supreme Court. O'Connor's seemingly soft stand on abortion caused some protest among strong conservatives. But during her confirmation hearings in the Senate, O'Connor explained that while she was personally against abortion, she had to put her beliefs aside when considering matters of law. She refused to answer any questions about

Sandra Day O'Connor is sworn in as the first female U.S. Supreme Court Justice on September 25, 1981.

how she might vote on any particular issue. The Judiciary Committee voted almost unanimously in her favor. The full Senate voted on September 22. O'Connor received ninety-one votes of approval; only eight voted against her, and one senator was absent. Three days later, O'Connor was a Supreme Court justice.

Over the years, O'Connor has voted on both sides of so-called conservative and liberal issues. She has supported states' rights (less power for the federal government), a typically conservative view. But she has also stood up, repeatedly, for freedom of information, the victims of sex discrimination, and the civil rights of all citizens. After many years on the Supreme Court, Sandra Day O'Connor continues to judge each case with careful thought, patience, a wide perspective, and a thorough understanding of the law. When not in Washington, she lives on the family ranch in Arizona with her husband. They have three grown sons.

Vigdis Finnbogadottir

Europe's First Woman
President
1930–

*V*igdis Finnbogadottir didn't have any overwhelming desire to run for president or any other political office in Iceland. Her love was the theater. And even there, she chose to remain offstage, instead helping to encourage and develop aspiring playwrights. But she was eventually convinced to try for her country's presidency. In 1980 she won the election, and although unaccustomed to being on stage, she won the hearts of her compatriots. She remained in office until 1996.

Vigdis Finnbogadottir was born April 15, 1930, in Reykjavík, Iceland's capital.

Her father was Finnbogi Rutur Thorvaldsson, a professor at the University of Iceland. Vigdis's mother, Sigridur Eiriksdottir, was a nurse and chaired the Icelandic Nurses Association for thirty-six years. In the small North Atlantic island nation of Iceland, a child's last name is formed by adding "sson" (for boys) or "dottir" (for girls) to the father's first name. This kind of naming system can be extremely confusing, even to the people who live there. So most Icelanders (even those prominent in society or politics) tend to use their first names.

After high school, Vigdis considered pursuing a career as a doctor but was drawn to the continent by the stories of European history and cultures she had heard from her parents. She completed junior college at Menntaskolinn in Reykjavík in 1949, then went to the University of Grenoble in France to study French. From there Vigdis attended the Sorbonne in Paris, where she studied literature and drama. Then it was on to Copenhagen, Denmark, for courses in theater history, and finally back to the University of Iceland to study English literature and education.

Vigdis began her career as a French teacher at the University of Iceland and then moved to an experimental school. Around the same time, she taught French on public television. During summer vacations, she worked as a tour guide for the Icelandic Tourist Bureau. She also joined an experimental theater group, the first ever established in Iceland.

In 1972, Vigdis was named director of the Reykjavík Theatre Company. Under her guidance, theater in Iceland achieved great success. She discovered writers, worked to have new plays translated and performed, and hosted a popular series on drama for the state-run television network. She also gave lectures on Icelandic culture. In 1978, she became chair of the Advisory Committee on Cultural Affairs in the Nordic Countries.

Throughout those years, Vigdis remained almost entirely nonpolitical. This fact, combined with her public identification with culture and the arts, made her a logical choice for the office of president. The presidency of Iceland is mostly a ceremonial position with little policy-making power. The purpose of the office is to help promote unity within the country by focusing public attention away from politics and back on national identity and culture. Vigdis did not even belong to a political party.

When approached by friends, Vigdis was unsure about running. She had never seen herself as a political leader. At the same time, she wanted to do something to advance the role of women in Iceland, who were strong and independent, yet were not treated as equal to men in the workplace. Vigdis was divorced and had became a single mother by adopting a daughter at the age of forty-one. Many voters saw her as a strong-willed, determined individual. Facing three popular male candidates, Vigdis campaigned aggressively for four months, a process that allowed her to meet and get to know the people of Iceland. She was elected on June 30, 1980. A month later, she became Iceland's fourth president since the nation won its independence from Denmark in 1944. She was reelected in 1984, 1988, and 1992.

As president, Vigdis assumed the responsibility of signing every bill passed by the Althing, the Icelandic parliament. Any bill she vetoed would go to the people for a vote, or referendum. The president of Iceland also oversees the transition of one government to the next, such as when a new prime minister is elected. And the president may be called upon to host summit meetings between the world's superpowers, such as the one involving U.S. president Ronald Reagan and Soviet president Mikhail Gorbachev in 1986. (Iceland has always been a peace-loving and neutral nation, and therefore the perfect setting for meetings between rivals.) But for the most part, President Vigdis spent her sixteen years in office building up the image of Iceland in the eyes of the world—and in the eyes of Icelanders.

Nancy Kassebaum

Groundbreaking
Senator from Kansas
1932–

As a young girl, Nancy Kassebaum used to sit and listen to the spirited political conversations that always filled her home. Her father was a two-term governor of Kansas, and he challenged Franklin D. Roosevelt for the presidency in 1936. After being sent up to bed, Nancy would continue listening to the muffled discussions through the heating vent. And she would imagine meeting, and perhaps even running against, well-known political figures of the day. As she got older, Nancy toyed with the idea of running for student offices in high school and college. But it took a sad turn of events in her marriage to motivate her to finally take the political plunge. Once she did, she grew into a solid senator from the nation's heartland. She was the first woman elected to the United States Senate who didn't follow in her husband's footsteps. And for the first two years of her tenure there, she was outnumbered by men, ninety-nine to one.

Nancy Landon was born on July 29, 1932, in Topeka, the capital of Kansas. Her parents were Alfred Mossman Landon and his second wife, Theo Cobb Landon. Alf Landon was a Republican Party legend of sorts, and he first planted the seed of political ambition in his daughter's mind. The very year Nancy was born, Alf was elected to the first of his two terms as governor of Kansas. Toward the end of his second term, he ran for president against Franklin Roosevelt. Although he collected just 8 electoral votes (to Roosevelt's 523), he never lost his love for politics.

After graduating from Topeka public schools, Nancy went off to the University of Kansas in Lawrence. There she earned a bachelor's degree in political science in 1954. Two years later, she studied at the University of Michigan, where she received her master's degree in diplomatic history. In 1956, Nancy married Philip Kassebaum, who had been her fellow student at the University of Kansas. Philip was a successful attorney and businessman from Wichita. After the couple settled down on a farm near the town of Maize, Kansas, Nancy focused mostly on her husband's career and their four children. But during that time she also worked as vice president of Kassebaum Communications, the operator of two radio stations. And she served on the Kansas Governmental Ethics Commission and was elected president of the Maize school board.

In 1975, the Kassebaums separated. Nancy took a job in the nation's capital as a caseworker for James Pearson, Republican senator from Kansas. In 1978, Senator Pearson decided not to run for reelection. Kassebaum carefully considered the possibilities, and after talking to family members and friends,

Senator Nancy Kassebaum of Kansas goes head to head with fellow Republican Senator Orrin Hatch of Utah over the wording of legislation that would make a woman's right to an abortion federal law. Kassebaum is strongly pro-choice, while Hatch is quite the opposite.

announced her candidacy. Alf Landon, for one, didn't think Kansas was ready for a woman senator. But Kassebaum won her party's nomination. In the general election, she faced Bill Roy, a Democrat who had nearly defeated Senator Bob Dole in their 1974 race. Kassebaum again prevailed, winning the election by about eighty-five thousand votes. Her victory in conservative Kansas made national headlines, partly because when she entered the Senate, she was the only woman there.

As a freshman senator, Kassebaum quietly went about learning how to do her job and how the system worked. She was appointed to several high-profile committees, including Banking, Housing, and Urban Affairs; Budget; Commerce, Science, and Transportation; and the Special Committee on Aging. The next year, she took a seat on the prestigious Foreign Relations Committee. Following the 1994 election, she served as chair of the Labor and Resources committee. As the only woman in the Senate, she was often wrongly perceived as a spokesperson for women's issues. In fact, her interests and concerns were wide-ranging. She was active in foreign affairs and worked to reduce the federal budget deficit. In 1992, she cofounded the Republican Majority Coalition in an attempt to reduce the influence of the religious right on party politics.

One of her greatest strengths was her ability—somewhat rare in politics—to clearly see both sides of an issue. The result was not a wishy-washy approach, but an open-minded perspective that led her to the decision she believed was right. She refused to simply vote along party lines, thereby maintaining access to both Republican and Democratic leaders throughout her three terms in office.

Nancy and Philip Kassebaum were divorced in 1979, the year the senator took office. She served in the United States Senate until 1997. After her last six-year term, she decided not to run for reelection but did agree to cochair a program aimed at campaign-finance reform.

Corazon Aquino

First Woman President
of the Philippines
1933–

*T*n the early 1980s, Corazon Aquino probably dreamed about the presidency of the Philippines. No doubt she imagined herself in the presidential palace, effecting reforms that would help the people of her country build better lives. But the president in those dreams would have been her husband, Benigno. His assassination in 1983 began nearly a decade of turbulence, exhilaration, fear, and accomplishment. And it paved the way to the presidential palace for his courageous widow.

Maria Corazon Cojuangco was born in Tarlac province on January 25, 1933. She was the sixth of eight children. Her parents, Demetria Sumulong and Jose "Pepe" Cojuangco, moved the family to the capital city of Manila when Cory was still a baby, so the older children could attend private school. The family had plenty of money in the bank, and politics in the blood: both of Cory's grandfathers had been senators, and Pepe was a congressman.

On December 8, 1941, the day after attacking Pearl Harbor, Japan invaded the Philippines. By the time World War II ended, Manila was almost completely destroyed. The Cojuangco family headed for the United States. They settled in New York, and although both of Cory's parents returned to Manila the following year, she and the other children stayed in America. When she was fourteen, Cory enrolled in the Notre Dame Convent School in New York City. After graduating, she attended the College of Mount St. Vincent in Riverdale, New York. Majoring in French and mathematics, Cory planned to become a teacher or translator. She was known as a good student, a devout Catholic, and a kind and charitable person. Every day, Cory walked to classes with a blind girl who lived in her dorm.

In Manila on vacation during her junior year, Cory became reacquainted with Benigno "Ninoy" Aquino. The pair had met years earlier, when they were nine, at a birthday party for Cory's father. Back then, the only thing they had in common was that both of their fathers were congressmen in Manila. Now Ninoy was a well-respected journalist for the *Manila Times*. When Cory returned to college, they corresponded through letters.

Meanwhile, Ninoy frequently dated another young woman, a distant relative named Imelda. She was a beauty queen, but tall for her age, so she was often neglected by young men at parties. Ninoy's aunt urged him to take Imelda out, and he did, introducing her to many of his friends. Nothing came of the relationship, but years later, their lives would intersect again in a dramatic way.

In 1953, Cory returned to the Philippines to attend law school at Manila's Far Eastern University. Ninoy and Cory were married on October 11, 1954, at a lavish affair with six hundred rich and politically powerful guests. After a honeymoon in the United States, the couple returned home, and Ninoy ran successfully for mayor of a small town called Concepcion. By 1959, when he was elected vice governor of Tarlac, the couple had two children. As Cory stayed in the background and took care of family matters, the outgoing Ninoy worked his way up through the thick jungle of Philippine politics. In 1961, Ninoy, running on the Liberal ticket, became the youngest person ever elected governor of Tarlac. Two years later, Ferdinand Marcos was elected president of the Philippines. His wife was a former beauty queen named Imelda.

In 1967, Ninoy became the country's youngest senator, as well as an outspoken critic of the Marcos administration. The years that followed were a time of great unrest. Protests, riots, bombings, and other violent acts were common in the Philippines. In 1972, Marcos imposed martial law. Ninoy was imprisoned and spent the next eight years in deplorable conditions behind bars. At one point, in 1977, he was sentenced to death by firing squad, but the execution never happened. Meanwhile, Cory stuck with him, bringing him encouragement and whatever comfort she could. As the years wore on, Cory began to appreciate the plight of the poor, the sick, and the underprivileged. She and her husband did what they could to keep the movement against Marcos alive. Then, in 1980, Ninoy was released to travel to Dallas for heart bypass surgery. He, Cory, and the children moved to the Boston area, where they lived for two years. Back in the Philippines, the opposition to Marcos was losing energy. Ninoy decided he must return, despite warnings of assassination plots against him.

On August 21, Ninoy said good-bye to Cory and boarded a plane at Boston's Logan Airport. Moments after landing in the Philippines, Ninoy stepped off the plane and was shot to death by assassins. A feeling of dread swept across the island nation.

In late 1985, Marcos called for an early election, and Cory was talked into running against him. The vote was held February 7, 1986, and Marcos was proclaimed the winner. However, rumors of election fraud spread quickly, and Cory began a nonviolent protest to force Marcos from office. Finally, after weeks of posturing and isolation, Ferdinand and Imelda Marcos left the Philippines for exile in the United States.

On February 25, 1986, Corazon Aquino became her nation's seventh president. The long, frustrating, and sometimes brutal road to the presidential palace had ended. A year later, a nationwide vote put her in office until 1992. Cory worked hard to reform the military, appointed many women to high positions in government, and helped form many nongovernmental organizations to advocate for the poor and underrepresented. She also survived several attempts to overthrow her government, including plots originating with Ferdinand Marcos.

Madeleine Kunin

First Woman Governor
of Vermont
1933–

By 1984, Vermont had been a state for a long time. It was the first new state created after the original thirteen colonies, joining the Union in 1791. In all that time, the people of Vermont had only elected two governors from the Democratic Party. They had never elected a Jew, and they had never elected a woman. So what chance did Madeleine Kunin have when she sought the highest office in that tradition-bound New England state?

Madeleine May was born on September 28, 1933, in Zurich, Switzerland. Her father, Ferdinand, was a German shoe importer. He died when Madeleine was three, leaving behind his Swiss wife, Renee, and two children. Three years later, Renee took the children to the United States to escape the growing threat of Hitler's Nazis. The ship that carried them to freedom was one of the last to leave Italy with Jews on board. Madeleine would later learn that at least five of her relatives perished in death camps.

Madeleine could speak no English when she left Europe, and her early years in Forest Hills, New York, were difficult. She chose to sit back, remain quiet, and observe. Her mother supported the family by working as a seamstress, French tutor, and babysitter. When Madeleine was in her teens, the Mays moved to Pittsfield, Massachusetts. After high school, she enrolled in the University of Massachusetts at Amherst, receiving her history degree, with honors, in 1956. Next, Madeleine attended Columbia University in New York City. After earning a master's degree in journalism, she was hired by the *Burlington Free Press*. Soon after, she met Arthur Kunin, a doctor. They were married in 1959. Madeleine continued to write and also worked as an assistant producer at a local television station. Their first child, Julia, was born in 1961. Over the next ten years, Peter, Adam, and Daniel were born, and Madeleine spent most of her time as wife and mother. Still, she worked with the League of Women Voters and in 1967 received another master's degree, this one in English literature from the University of Vermont. In 1970, the family traveled to Switzerland. There Madeleine met women's activists who were struggling to win the vote for Swiss women. Inspired by their activism, Madeleine returned to the United States eager to "make a difference" in the world of politics.

It was 1972, and Madeleine headed for the Vermont state capital to break into the political arena. But her first attempt was not successful. She missed becoming Burlington's first woman alderman (elected city official) by sixteen votes. The following year, she was elected as a Democrat to the Vermont house of representatives. Her campaign addressed issues related to education, the environment, and the state's poor. By her third two-year term, she was the chair of the powerful appropriations committee, which made decisions about state spending.

In 1978, Kunin ran for the office of lieutenant governor, defeating her Republican opponent with a little over 50 percent of the vote. Two years later, she won reelection with nearly 60 percent of the ballots cast. During this time, Kunin had been a devoted student of government and politics, and had learned a great deal. Most important, she had learned to go out and meet the people and talk to them about their concerns. The quiet little immigrant girl had grown up and overcome her fears.

In 1982, when Richard Snelling announced that he would not seek a third term as governor, Kunin declared herself a candidate. Then Snelling changed his mind, and Vermont's voters, typically loyal to incumbents, elected him again. But Kunin ran an effective and impressive campaign, winning 44 percent of the vote. In 1984 (Vermont's governor serves two-year terms), she came back to defeat John Easton, a former state attorney general, in a very close race.

As governor, Kunin appointed a record number of women to state office. Her five-person cabinet had two women. The man she hired to be her press secretary had been an outspoken critic of Kunin's performance as lieutenant governor (she didn't want to hear only agreement). Her first real test came when she had to stand up to the state's powerful ski industry after some resorts tried to ignore Vermont's strict environmental laws. The governor remained firm, and environmentalists praised her for it. After eighteen months, Kunin also had erased a thirty-five million dollar deficit. And she did it while increasing the state education budget by 25 percent. She also got the legislature to pass even stricter environmental laws.

During her second term, which began after a narrow 1986 victory, Kunin grew even more comfortable with her constituents. Wherever she went in the state, people called her "Madeleine," rather than "Governor." Kunin was elected to a third term in 1988. She continued to work for improved child-care programs, more opportunity for women, and better support for families, the elderly, and the disadvantaged.

Kunin decided that her third term as governor would be her last. In 1990, she assembled staff, colleagues, and friends to say good-bye. Then she went home with Arthur, confident that she had done her best for the people of Vermont. As one of the first woman governors, she had also accomplished much for women everywhere.

Ann Richards

First Woman Governor
of Texas
1933–

A nn Richards emerged from a rural town in east-central Texas with a quick wit and a gift for hard-hitting speech. She climbed the political ladder in Texas, not an easy accomplishment for a woman, and reached for the highest office in the state. She was the keynote speaker at the Democratic National Convention. She was in Dallas when President Kennedy was assassinated. She has battled alcoholism and survived divorce. She has won elections, and she has lost elections. And every step of the way, she has touched the people around her.

Dorothy Ann Willis was born in Lakeview, Texas, on September 1, 1933.

She grew up as the only child of Cecil Willis, a truck driver, and Iona Warren Willis. Both parents came from farming families, and they never had quite enough money to make ends meet. But Cecil and Iona made sure their daughter benefited from speech and piano lessons. Her father encouraged her to always question injustice and to search for its solution. And he convinced her that she could accomplish whatever she set her mind to. Those lessons would serve her well in the world of politics.

Dorothy Ann attended Theodore Roosevelt Junior High School in San Diego, where her father was stationed in the navy. After World War II, the family returned to Lakeview, and Dorothy Ann entered the local public school. After the Willises moved to Waco, Dorothy Ann enrolled in the high school as Ann Willis, dropping her first name in order to sound less like a farm girl. (Waco, it seemed to her, was a big, sophisticated city.) She excelled in English and speech. After graduation in 1950, Ann received debating scholarships from several colleges. Her parents convinced her to attend Baylor University in Waco. In 1953, at the end of her junior year, Ann married David Richards, a longtime boyfriend. She received her degree in speech and government in 1954, then enrolled at the University of Texas at Austin to work on her teacher's certificate.

From 1955 to 1957, Ann taught government and history at Fulmore Junior High School in Austin. In 1959, Ann and David had their first child, Cecile, and the family moved to Dallas, where David had been named Democratic precinct chairman. Ann helped found an organization called the North Dallas Democratic Women and was soon serving as its president. In 1960, she worked for the Kennedy-Johnson presidential campaign. (In November 1963, Ann was seated at a luncheon awaiting an appearance by President Kennedy when she learned he had been shot.) Later in the decade, she helped organize the Dallas Committee for Peaceful Integration and worked for the Dallas chapter of the NAACP.

In 1975, local Democrats asked David to run for county commissioner. When he declined, they asked Ann to run. In 1976, she became the first woman commissioner of Travis County. Richards implemented a program to assist parents raising children born with birth defects. She established a rape crisis center, as well as a haven for battered women. But as Richards was working to improve the lives of other women, she was apparently neglecting her own. As she grew more politically active, the demands began to show on her marriage. And as the marriage suffered, she turned to alcohol for comfort. Richards checked herself into a rehabilitation facility in Minneapolis in late 1980. However, she and David could not reconcile, and they soon separated.

In 1981, Richards was named Woman of the Year by the Texas Women's Political Caucus. She also served on President Jimmy Carter's Advisory Committee on Women and lobbied for the Equal Rights Amendment. She was elected state treasurer in 1982, even though the issue of her drinking problem had been raised during the campaign—an issue she deflected with grace and candor. In office, Richards revamped the state's outdated record-keeping system, installing computers, check-coding machines, and other modern equipment. Her efforts saved Texas millions of dollars. In the presidential election year of 1984, she was chosen to second the nomination of Walter Mondale, and she advised him on his planned selection of Geraldine Ferraro as his running mate. In 1986, she was reelected state treasurer, without opposition, becoming the first woman to serve back-to-back terms in Texas state politics. Two years later, she was the keynote speaker at the Democratic National Convention in Atlanta, where she described Vice President George Bush as having been born "with a silver foot in his mouth."

Republican governor William Clements Jr. retired in 1990, and Richards decided his vacant office was her next stop. Again fighting the alcoholism issue—and unsubstantiated accusations of past drug abuse—Richards shot back with tough campaign ads. She won the nomination and then faced the Republican, Clayton Williams. Richards's prochoice stand on abortion attracted votes from many Republican women. She pulled off the upset and headed to the governor's office.

As governor, Richards dealt with hazardous waste disposal, the reduction of state agencies, and questionable insurance practices. She appointed women, African-Americans, and Hispanics in large numbers, just as she had done as state treasurer. She streamlined spending, reduced waste, and increased manufacturing jobs to record numbers. Crime rates dropped and education improved. She was a popular governor. But Richards was caught in the anti-incumbent mood that swept across America in 1994: she lost a close race to George W. Bush, the ex-president's son.

Ann and David Richards were divorced in 1984. They have four grown children. The former governor travels a great deal to speak to women and girls about politics, power, and their role in the system. She also enjoys being a grandmother and riding her motorcycle.

Jane Byrne

First Woman
Mayor of Chicago
1934–

*J*ane Byrne had never held a political office. She entered the campaign with just one hundred thousand dollars, a fraction of the money backing her opponent. She had been fired from her job as commissioner of consumer sales. She was not part of the political machine. Her opponent was the incumbent mayor. And no woman had ever been elected mayor of Chicago. Was there any chance for Jane Byrne to take command of what was then the second largest city in the United States?

The second of six children, Jane Margaret Burke was born on May 24, 1934, on the north side of Chicago, Illinois. Born between two brothers, Jane competed with them in baseball, basketball, swimming, and horseback riding. In the process, she developed the attitude that if the boys could do it, so could she. Jane attended Queen of All Saints elementary school and Saint Scholastica High School. Then she enrolled in Barat College of the Sacred Heart in Lake Forest, a Chicago suburb. She majored in chemistry and biology and received her bachelor's degree in 1955. Jane abandoned her goal of becoming a doctor when she married William P. Byrne on December 31, 1956. Exactly one year later, their daughter, Kathy, was born. When William joined the Marine Corps, the Byrnes moved to the Cherry Point Marine Corps Air Station in North Carolina. Jane and Kathy went to Chicago to visit family and friends in May 1959. William, now a pilot, flew up to join them several weeks later, but he was killed when his plane crashed in heavy fog.

In the spring of 1960, Jane heard a speech by presidential candidate John F. Kennedy. She was moved to visit his Chicago campaign headquarters and offer her services as a volunteer. She was soon hired as the secretary-treasurer of Kennedy's Chicago organization. Several Kennedy staffers were impressed by Jane's work ethic, and after he was elected the new president invited her to work for him in Washington. She declined the offer, preferring to stay in Chicago with her daughter. Jane earned a teaching certificate and for the next two years worked as a substitute teacher in Chicago's public schools.

Jane kept in touch with the Kennedys, and the president invited her to attend the Army-Air Force football game in Chicago in the fall of 1963. Kennedy could not be there, but Jane was noticed among the presidential aides by the mayor of Chicago, Richard J. Daley. The following year, Daley spoke with Byrne about her future. He admired her style and urged her to gain some political experience. Later in 1964, the mayor appointed Byrne to a minor position in a federal antipoverty program. She toiled there for the next four years, learning the system and its players. In 1968, Daley named Byrne the commissioner of consumer sales, weights, and measures. She was the first woman in his cabinet.

Byrne immediately went after the corrupt elements in her department, firing several staff members. She implemented numerous reforms to protect consumers, including a new meat-grading system and a ban on phosphate detergents. She went after the city's taxi drivers, auto mechanics, and gas station proprietors, establishing herself as a tough, no-nonsense consumer advocate. Under Mayor Daley's guidance, she learned how to control her timing, and her temper. In the process, she became a skilled politician who could accomplish her objectives without making enemies. She also remained fiercely loyal to Daley.

In the spring of 1975, Daley suffered a stroke. Byrne angrily accused some city aldermen of plotting to succeed him. She called them, among other things, "political vultures," a phrase they did not soon forget. Daley recovered from the stroke and in 1975 named Byrne cochair of the Cook County Democratic Central Committee. The following year, however, Daley died. He was succeeded by Michael A. Bilandic. Byrne had no real political power, and the men she had verbally attacked now banded together to remove her from her position as cochair of the Democratic Central Committee. Meanwhile, Byrne was also having problems with the new mayor. When, as commissioner of consumer sales, she accused him of fraudulent activity after a city taxi fare increase in 1977, he fired her.

On March 17, 1978, Jane Byrne married Jay McMullen, a journalist. That same year she announced she would challenge Bilandic for the mayor's office in the 1979 elections. Few political experts gave her much chance of getting the nomination over Bilandic, but Byrne campaigned furiously. She accused the mayor of blatant dishonesty. She pointed out to voters the deterioration of city services. And she proclaimed herself Mayor Daley's rightful heir. Then nature took a crack at Michael Bilandic. On New Year's Eve, snow began to fall, and by the time it stopped, drifts as deep as eight feet had buried the city. Snow removal was slow, garbage removal was halted, transportation was blocked, and Bilandic's approval rating dropped drastically. On February 27, 1979, more than eight hundred thousand Chicago voters turned out at the polls. Byrne won the primary by fifteen thousand votes. In the April election, Byrne captured 82 percent of the vote and all fifty city wards.

As mayor, Byrne set out to enhance the city's efficiency, even while cutting the budget. She trimmed and reorganized Chicago's police and sanitation departments, firing top officials and unneeded employees. Four years later, Byrne was challenged by Richard M. Daley, the son of her former mentor, and Chicago politician Harold Washington. Byrne and Daley split the white vote, and Washington captured virtually all of the African-American vote. Washington was elected.

In 1987, Byrne again lost to Washington in the primary. Four years later, she failed once more to win the Democratic nomination, this time losing to Richard M. Daley, the new mayor.

Edith Cresson

France's Fighting
Prime Minister
1934–

*E*dith Cresson has land-ed more than her share of political jobs. In the process, she has been labeled with more than her share of nicknames. In a country in which women only acquired the right to vote and hold public office in 1944, Cresson has a long record of public service. And the scars to prove it.

Edith Campion was born on January 27, 1934, in Boulogne-Billancourt, just outside Paris. Her parents were Gabriel, a tax inspector, and Jacqueline (Vignal) Campion. She has a younger brother, Harold. Edith learned English from her British nanny. When France was overtaken by the Nazis in 1940, Edith's father settled his wife and children in Switzerland and then went back to Paris. Edith attended a convent boarding school near Lake Geneva. The Campions returned to France after World War II. Edith earned a business degree at *L'Ecole des Hautes Etudes Commerciales.* She then earned a doctorate in demography with a dissertation on the life of women in a rural area of France. By then she had begun to separate herself from the affluence of the Campion family's upper-middle-class existence.

In 1959, Edith married Jacques Cresson, a Peugeot automobile executive. Her earliest political activities were conservative, but she moved left in 1965 when she met François Mitterand, leader of the Democratic and Socialist Resistance Union. Mitterand challenged Charles de Gaulle for the presidency that year, losing by a slim margin. Nevertheless, the Mitterand-Cresson team had been formed. He called her "my little soldier." In 1971, Mitterand was elected first secretary of the Socialist Party. Four years later, he helped nominate Cresson to the party. After joining, she was immediately named national party secretary in charge of youth organization. In October, she ran for a seat in the National Assembly. Although she lost, she impressed many political observers with her spirited and energetic campaign and earned the new nickname "la battante," which means "the fighter."

Cresson was elected mayor of Thuré in 1977. Two years later, she won a seat in the European Parliament and was quickly appointed to the Agricultural Commission. When Mitterand was elected president of France in 1981, he named Cresson head of the Ministry of Agriculture. She was the first woman to hold that job. The country's farmers, who were generally conservative, could not adjust to a woman minister and reacted harshly to Cresson's appointment. They called her "the perfumed one," "La Parisienne," and other less flattering names. She was ridiculed during protests, pelted with tomatoes, and on at least one occasion, had to be taken away by helicopter from a menacing crowd. Despite the farmers' lack of affection for her,

Cresson continued to promote French agricultural products on the world market and called for increased sales to Third World nations.

In 1983, Cresson was the only Socialist to unseat a Conservative when she was elected mayor of her new hometown, Châtellerault. Later that year, she was named France's minister of trade and tourism. During the next three years, Cresson looked for ways to modernize her nation's industry. She also devoted herself to promoting French products, both at home and while traveling in other countries. She rode French motor scooters to and from work, emphasizing her belief that the models produced in France were as good as those made in Japan. And she publicized French fashions by wearing clothes, on loan from her country's leading designers, to trade shows abroad. (Cresson was known, briefly, as "the Madonna of Small Business.")

As trade minister, Cresson directed the revitalization of France's steel industry. She pushed for low-interest loans and lower taxes for businesses and simplified the process for starting a business or acquiring a patent. She also dramatically reduced France's trade deficit.

In 1986, Cresson was again elected to the National Assembly. Two years later, she was appointed to the cabinet of Prime Minister Michel Rocard as his minister for European affairs. Shortly afterward, during a 1990 visit to Paris by Japan's prime minister, Cresson issued a statement strongly critical of that country's trade practices. "Japan is an adversary that doesn't play by the rules," she said, "and has an absolute desire to conquer the world." The resulting public outcry against her statements caused her to resign in October of that year.

Cresson worked in private industry for the next six months. Then, in May 1991, President Mitterand asked her to replace Prime Minister Rocard, who was thought to be planning his own run for the presidency. Cresson accepted, amid the cries and protests of the opposition. Even many impartial

Edith Cresson, then prime minister of France, poses here with Russian president Boris Yeltsin shortly before her resignation in April 1992.

observers felt Cresson would create more problems than she solved. Meanwhile, the new prime minister set out to improve productivity, build demand for French products, and reduce unemployment. But in June 1991, unemployment in France stood at nearly 10 percent, the economy was stalled, and violence in the cities was on the rise. Support for the Mitterand government was slipping. Cresson continued to loudly criticize Japanese industry, threatening the relationship Mitterand had been building with Japan, and further weakening her own popularity.

With her approval rating deteriorating and her skills and experience overlooked by the French media and her colleagues in government, Cresson was asked to step down. She resigned as prime minister in April 1992. She had broken new ground in French government, and had blown up some political bridges in the process. Cresson is now president of a Paris consulting firm. She and her husband, Jacques, have two daughters.

Geraldine Ferraro

First Woman Vice
Presidential Nominee
1935–

As a three-term congresswoman from New York, Geraldine Ferraro certainly accomplished a great deal for her constituents, and for the country as a whole. But she will always be remembered as the first woman nominated by a major political party for the office of vice president of the United States.

Geraldine Anne Ferraro was born in Newburgh, New York, on August 26, 1935. She was named after her brother, Gerard, who had died at the age of three. Her father, who had immigrated to America from Italy, died when Geraldine was eight. Following his death, the rest of the family moved to New

York City. In 1956, Geraldine graduated from Marymount Manhattan College with a bachelor of arts degree. She taught English in the public schools and, in 1960, earned her law degree at Fordham University, where she was one of 2 women in the class of 179 students. That same year she married John Zaccaro, a real-estate developer.

In 1961, Ferraro was admitted to the New York State bar and began working part-time as a lawyer in her husband's firm. In 1974, she was named assistant district attorney in Queens County. The following year, she joined the newly formed Special Victims Bureau, which prosecuted cases involving abuse of women, children, and the elderly. She was soon named head of the bureau.

Then, in 1978, the congressman from Ferraro's Queens district retired, and Ferraro announced that she would run for his vacant seat. Local party leaders discouraged her candidacy and did little to support her. But Ferraro proved to be a tough and tireless campaigner. She won the election by a 10 percent margin. Her victories in each of the next two elections were even more substantial, firmly establishing her as a formidable politician in the eyes of New York voters, and as a winner in the minds of Democrats everywhere.

Ferraro slipped easily into the role of congresswoman. She played by the House rules and was considered "one of the guys" by most of her colleagues. Speaker of the House Tip O'Neill appointed her to the Democratic Steering and Policy Committee and the all-powerful Budget Committee and made her secretary of the House Democratic Caucus. Ferraro was well aware that in many cases she was being treated as the token woman on these committees. Nevertheless, she accepted the appointments as a way to get in the door, then took full advantage of the opportunities to establish her own power and influence. Behind the scenes, Ferraro spent countless hours listening to debates, asking questions, and studying transcripts of hearings in order to learn more about the issues affecting the people she represented.

When Walter Mondale, shown here, asked Geraldine Ferraro to be his running mate for the 1984 presidential elections, she made history as the first woman to run for vice president.

Ferraro was instrumental in getting money from Washington for New York City's water tunnel project. She paid special attention to the needs of her ethnically diverse district, such as establishing a hotline to convey news about conditions in Poland, which was experiencing great upheaval at the time. And as always, she was actively involved in legislation benefiting women, children, and the elderly. She usually voted with her party, but on certain issues, went her own way. For example, she voted for tuition tax credits for private schools, while opposing mandatory busing. She also came out against funding the rebels in Nicaragua and disagreed with many of President Reagan's economic policies.

Her record was solid, and her reputation was spreading. Geraldine Ferraro had gained the respect of her constituents, peers, and opponents. She was enjoying her career and looking forward to future successes. But she could not have imagined the stage she was about to step onto, or the role she was about to play.

In November 1983, a small group of women, including Ferraro's administrative assistant, invited her out to dinner to discuss the possibility of a woman running for vice president. They had compiled a list of women and concluded that Ferraro was the best choice. Walter Mondale, the certain presidential nominee, would soon be interviewing candidates for the slot. They wanted to push for her selection and asked if she'd work with them. Believing her chances of actually being chosen were next to zero, she agreed. But on July 9, Mondale called Ferraro and asked the question: "Will you be my running mate?"

Many believe that simple request forever changed the future of politics in the United States. It certainly changed Geraldine Ferraro's life. The novelty of a woman actually running for vice president—and possibly being "a heartbeat away from the presidency"—forced the entire nation to reexamine itself and the political process. Ferraro was asked questions ranging from her willingness to push the nuclear button to her ability to bake a blueberry muffin. The press scrutinized her smile, her hair, the way she dressed. Most excruciating, however, was the relentless probe into her husband's financial dealings and possible links to organized crime. It was a rigorous summer and fall for Ferraro, filled with harsh questions and the stress that always comes with setting a precedent. But by most estimates, she ran a refreshing and professional campaign. Many political experts said she won her debate with Vice President George Bush. And wherever she went throughout the country, crowds greeted her with enthusiasm.

In the end, it may be that no Democratic ticket in 1984 was going to defeat Reagan and Bush. But Ferraro's nomination and her performance paved the way for the future. She later summed it up: "I don't think the press will be looking to see if the next female candidate will burst out crying every time she has a press conference. . . . Perhaps the style of her campaign will be less important and the substance of her campaign will get the attention it deserves."

Ferraro entered the race for U.S. senator from New York in 1992, but lost in the primary. Six years later, she announced plans to run again for the Senate.

Barbara Jordan

First African-American Woman to Preside Over a Legislature 1936–1996

There was a time, in the mid-1970s, when a large number of people believed Barbara Jordan would become the first African-American—and the first female—governor of Texas, Speaker of the House, Supreme Court justice, vice president, or even president. Such was the range of her abilities, the depth of her intellect, and the power of her reputation among political leaders and the American public. In the end, Jordan decided that someday other qualified people would be those groundbreakers, but it wouldn't be Barbara Jordan. She wanted to teach.

Barbara Charline Jordan was born February 21, 1936, in Houston, Texas. She was the youngest of three daughters born to Benjamin and Arlyne (Patten) Jordan. Benjamin was a minister at the Good Hope Missionary Baptist Church. Arlyne spoke often at her husband's services and was widely respected for her oratory skills. Barbara's family was poor, but both parents instilled in her the confidence that she could accomplish great things. Toward that end, they made education the highest priority. After graduating in the top 5 percent of her high school class in 1952, Jordan attended Texas Southern University. In 1956, she was the first African-American student at Boston University Law School, where she earned her law degree in 1959. After passing the Massachusetts bar exam, she headed back to Texas and began a private law practice in Houston. Jordan also worked as an administrative assistant for a county judge, which sparked her interest in politics. Then, in 1960, she became involved in John F. Kennedy's presidential campaign. After his victory, she realized political action might be the way to improve the lives of African-Americans.

Jordan campaigned for a seat in the Texas House of Representatives in 1962 and 1964, losing both times. Then, in 1966, Jordan defeated J. C. Whitfield to become the first African-American state senator in Texas since 1863. Sitting among her thirty white male colleagues, Jordan realized that to be a black congresswoman in Texas in the 1960s was a remarkable accomplishment. But her goals went far beyond issues of race or gender. During her years in the state legislature, she worked hard for reform in the areas of housing, employment, and voter registration. On March 28, 1972, Jordan was elected president pro tem of the state legislature. She was thus the first African-American woman in American history to preside over a lawmaking body. In 1972, Jordan became the first black woman elected to the United States House of Representatives from the Deep South (Shirley Chisholm had done it in New York four years earlier). Jordan quickly earned the trust and respect of a wider audience in Texas, and she was reelected in 1974 and 1976.

In 1974, Jordan's reputation reached the national level when she was one of only two women serving on the House Judiciary Committee during the Watergate hearings. It was Jordan who began the committee's public deliberations when she delivered a speech concerning the possible impeachment of President Richard Nixon. She remained a key figure throughout that process. But it wasn't until two years later, as a keynote speaker at the Democratic National Convention, that Jordan firmly established herself as a political star. "My presence here," she said that night, "is one additional bit of evidence that the American dream need not forever be deferred. What we see today is simply a dress rehearsal for the day and time we meet in convention to nominate Madam President." Her resonant voice, confident manner, and powerful intellect excited the crowd and impressed the nation. Soon, Jordan's name was being mentioned in conversations related to future Supreme Court nominees and Texas gubernatorial candidates. Or perhaps she would stay in Congress and be elected Speaker of the House. Or maybe she'd be chosen as a vice presidential candidate. Or she might even run for president herself. The possibilities seemed endless.

However, in 1977, as Jordan began her third term as a U.S. representative, she decided that politics was not her final destiny. She announced that she would not run for a fourth term. The country would soon be ready for African-American women to fill the roles she had been mentioned for, she reasoned, but it was not quite ready yet. She had things to do and did not want to spend the rest of her life struggling in vain to make something happen before its time.

In 1982, Jordan became a professor at the Lyndon B. Johnson School of Public Affairs at the University of Texas in Austin, teaching courses in government policy. Eight years later, she also headed the Commission on Immigration Reform.

Jordan died on January 17, 1996. Many of her accomplishments were distinguished by the fact that she was the first African-American woman to achieve them. But perhaps her greatest accomplishment was what she did to ensure that she wouldn't be the last.

Barbara Mikulski

Maryland's Champion
of the Working Class
1936–

Growing up in the streets of Baltimore, Barbara Mikulski saw and lived among hardworking, law-abiding citizens. They were people who paid their taxes, took care of their kids, and went to church on Sundays. But gradually things began to change, and not for the better. Neighborhoods were crumbling. The harder people worked, the less they had to show for it. The small businesses that helped build America were being swept aside. Crime was on the rise. Worst of all, the solutions to many of the problems were within reach, but the system designed to produce those solutions just wasn't functioning. What was needed was someone to step into that system and untie the knots, relay the messages, and make things happen. It would have to be someone who knew the culture of the streets, and who could learn the language of government.

Barbara Ann Mikulski was born on July 20, 1936, in Baltimore, Maryland. She grew up in Highlandtown, an ethnically diverse, working-class neighborhood. Her parents, William and Christine Kutz Mikulski, ran a small grocery store called Willy's Market. Barbara attended the Sacred Heart of Jesus elementary school. In 1954, she graduated from the Institute of Notre Dame High School. She thought about becoming a nun but changed her mind and went to Mount Saint Agnes College (now part of Loyola University) to study medical technology. Then she changed her mind again, switching over to social work. In 1958, she graduated with a bachelor's degree in sociology. Mikulski then became a caseworker for several social work agencies in Baltimore. Meanwhile, she did graduate studies in the evenings. In 1965, she received a master's degree in social work from the University of Maryland. She then taught at the VISTA training center until 1970 and became involved in various community projects. "The more I worked with people on a one-to-one basis," she said, "the more I saw that institutions were really the problem."

As Mikulski spoke to people in her old neighborhood, including her own family members, she realized that social programs were causing ethnic groups to grow apart. Each group thought the others were getting more. The truth was, nobody was getting enough, and everyone was growing resentful. Mikulski began to think about coalition politics—bringing different groups together to use their collective strength in working toward common goals. She also started to understand the value and beauty of ethnic diversity, even as so many around her were becoming "Americanized" and trying to forget where their families came from. She became an associate of the

National Center for Urban Ethnic Affairs, as well as a member of the Polish Women's Alliance.

When Robert F. Kennedy and Martin Luther King Jr. were assassinated within months of each other in 1968, Mikulski decided to change her life. And she decided to do it through politics. She moved back to her old neighborhood and helped start a community organization that successfully blocked harmful construction projects, while implementing positive changes. As she began to understand the problems in the neighborhoods, Mikulski also realized she could help a lot more if she was inside the system. In 1971, she won a seat on the Baltimore City Council. She used her position to help rape victims, the elderly, and other seemingly powerless groups. In 1972, she was a special adviser to vice presidential candidate R. Sargent Shriver. Mikulski dedicated herself to rebuilding the Democratic Party and motivating more women to run for high elected office. In 1974, she decided to run for the United States Senate against Republican incumbent Charles Mathias Jr. She lost a hard-fought election but in the process won an impressive 43 percent of the vote.

In 1975, Mikulski was reelected to the Baltimore City Council. A year later, she ran for the vacant Third Congressional District seat in the House of Representatives. She took 75 percent of the vote, then went to Washington, where she quickly established herself as a smart politician. Mikulski was reelected to the House four consecutive times. Then, in 1986, Mathias retired, and Mikulski ran for the Senate again, this time winning easily.

Mikulski has long been an advocate for the environment, supporting strict guidelines for the disposal of hazardous waste. She has also pushed for increased government funding of health care programs, and for laws ending discrimination in the workplace. She has fought for women, the elderly, workers, consumers, and just about anyone else who can be considered an underdog in society. Mikulski understands the problems of middle-class ethnic neighborhoods. She knows the system contains the answers to those problems. And she is willing to do the work to bring answer and problem together, just as she has worked to bring different groups together to fight for a common objective.

Barbara Mikulski was reelected to the Senate in 1992. She is considered the dean of women in the Senate and acts as mentor for many of them.

1992: Year of the Woman

*E*leven women ran for election to the United States Senate in 1992, a record. Barbara Mikulski was reelected from Maryland, and four new female senators claimed their places: Dianne Feinstein and Barbara Boxer took both seats in California, Carol Moseley-Braun won in Illinois, and Patty Murray was elected in Washington. That brought the number of women in the Senate from two to six (including Nancy Kassebaum from Kansas).

On the other side of the Capitol, 106 women ran for seats in the House of Representatives. Enough won to boost the number of female representatives, overnight, from twenty-eight to forty-seven.

What caused this surge in the number of women running for Congress? One factor was the large percentage of male incumbents who retired. But, clearly, the Clarence Thomas hearings also played a major role.

Clarence Thomas had been selected by President George Bush in 1991 to become the newest member of the U.S. Supreme Court. All nominees to the Supreme Court must be approved by a vote of the Senate. This vote takes place after confirmation hearings, in which members of the Senate Judiciary

Barbara Boxer and Dianne Feinstein were both elected to Congress in 1992. Many believe that the Clarence Thomas confirmation hearings played a major role in the record number of women who sought elected office that year.

Committee question the nominee about his or her background, attitudes, and beliefs. During the Thomas hearings, which took place in the fall of 1991, a law professor named Anita Hill testified that Thomas had sexually harassed her when the two worked together at a government agency. The testimony went on for days and included graphic language that seemed out of place in the hallowed halls of Congress and the Supreme Court.

The fourteen members of the Judiciary Committee were all men. As portrayed on television to a mesmerized national audience, they seemed con-

Anita Hill testifies before a Senate confirmation panel during the Clarence Thomas hearings in October 1991.

fused, insensitive, and out of touch. Many later confessed that they didn't understand the seriousness of the allegations until they went home and heard what their wives had to say. In the end, the Senate confirmed Thomas, and he became a judge on the highest court in the land. Women across the country were infuriated by what they perceived as one men's club (the Senate) trying to protect an incoming member of another men's club (the Supreme Court). Many of the women who ran for office in 1992 no doubt made their decision either during or shortly after the Thomas hearings.

It is interesting to note that during his final testimony at the hearings, Thomas also lashed out at the senators, claiming they were hounding him in what he described as a "high-tech lynching." We may never know who was telling the truth about Thomas's alleged sexual harassment of Hill. But we do know that the United States Congress turned a corner in 1992. Since then, female representation in Congress has held steady at an all-time high of 11 percent. In 1997, nine women held seats in the Senate and fifty in the House.

Dianne Feinstein

Tough and Sensitive
Mayor and Senator
1933–

*D*ianne Feinstein had run for mayor of San Francisco twice and lost both times. Yet when she finally did become mayor in 1978, it was not with the exhilaration that normally accompanies victory. Her husband had recently died of cancer. Her trip to the Himalayas that followed his death had been cut short when she got seriously ill. And now she had been appointed mayor after her predecessor was assassinated. Perhaps most difficult of all, her appointment by the board of supervisors had been made necessary by the violent act of one of its own members. The city needed a mayor of enormous strength. Did Feinstein have enough left?

Dianne Emiel Goldman was born June 22, 1933, in San Francisco, California. She was the eldest of Leon and Betty Goldman's three daughters. Dianne attended San Francisco public schools through eighth grade, then went to Convent of the Sacred Heart High School, where she graduated in 1951. She went on to Stanford University, earning a bachelor of arts degree in history and serving as student body vice president.

In 1956, Dianne married Jack Berman, a prosecutor in the San Francisco district attorney's office. Their daughter, Katherine Anne, was born the following year. The couple divorced in 1959. In 1962, she married Dr. Bertram Feinstein, director of the Neurological Institute at Mt. Zion Hospital and Medical Center.

Dianne worked as a volunteer for John F. Kennedy's presidential campaign in 1960. She then served as a member of the California Women's Board of Terms and Parole until 1966. She was also a member of the Mayor's Committee on Crime in San Francisco and chaired the San Francisco Committee on Adult Detention. During this time Dianne developed a belief that capital punishment was wrong, a belief that would change in later years.

In 1968, San Francisco Mayor Joseph Alioto appointed Feinstein to a blue-ribbon committee on crime. The following year, she set out to win a seat on the board of supervisors. Despite the discouragement of the political experts, and the fact that no woman had been elected to the board in forty-eight years, Feinstein received more votes than any other candidate. In the process, she automatically became the first woman ever elected president of the board. She would hold that office for three terms. During her tenure, Feinstein pushed for an increase in the number of police officers patrolling the neighborhoods. She also worked to limit the spread of pornography and defended the rights of gays and lesbians. Inspired by her success and popularity, Feinstein challenged Alioto for the mayor's office in 1971. But she was hurt by her support of busing and a city income tax. She lost badly in the election.

Four years later, Feinstein launched another campaign for mayor. This time she lost to Senator George Moscone, who was elected with 40 percent of the vote. In 1977, Feinstein was again elected president of the board. It was a violent time around the country, but especially in San Francisco. And it was a difficult time, personally, for Feinstein. An assassination attempt was made against President Gerald Ford during a visit to the city in 1975. And Feinstein herself was attacked several times, once with a bomb planted in her home. Her father died in 1975. Her second husband died in 1978.

During the fall of 1978, Feinstein had made up her mind to retire from politics. She conveyed that decision to a news reporter on November 27. A few hours later, she became the first woman mayor of San Francisco when George Moscone and supervisor Harvey Milk were shot to death in their offices. The assassinations threw the city into a state of shock and turmoil, and Feinstein faced a difficult task. The man who shot Moscone and Milk was a member of the board of supervisors who had recently resigned. Nine days before the murders, Jim Jones led nine hundred cult members in a mass suicide in Guyana. Jim Jones had, just two years earlier, been named San Francisco's housing commissioner. More than ever, the city needed a mayor who could be sensitive and tough at the same time.

Feinstein proved to be the right person at the right time. Her leadership inspired San Francisco to bounce back. In 1979, Feinstein was elected mayor in her own right and moved quickly to beef up the police force and improve city services. After winning again in 1983, Feinstein was considered as a possible running mate by Democratic presidential nominee Walter Mondale. During her second full term, Feinstein worked to build up the city's AIDS support services but angered many gay activists by shutting down the city's bath-houses, which were popular meeting places for gay men.

San Francisco has a two-term limit for its mayor, so Feinstein had to leave office in 1988. She decided the governor's house should be her next residence. After capturing the Democratic nomination, however, she lost to Republican senator Pete Wilson in the 1990 general election. Wilson appointed a consultant named John Seymour to temporarily take over his Senate seat. But in a special 1992 election, Feinstein defeated Seymour to finish out Wilson's term. She was reelected to a full six-year term in 1994.

As a senator, Feinstein has worked to limit the manufacture and sale of semiautomatic weapons and has proposed legislation to stop illegal immigration. She has also helped establish two national parks and one national preserve in California. She has served on numerous Senate committees, including Judiciary, Foreign Relations, and Rules and Administration Committees. Since 1980, Feinstein has been married to Richard Blum, an investment banker.

Barbara Boxer

Women's Advocate in the House and Senate 1940–

arbara Boxer grew up with sexual discrimination. She had endured it throughout her career. After watching the Clarence Thomas hearings on television, she decided it was her destiny to help change things for the better.

Barbara Levy was born on November 11, 1940, in Brooklyn, New York. Her parents were Ira R. and Sophie (Silvershein) Levy. As a young child, Barbara did not exhibit the kind of strong-willed spirit that later characterized her. But by the time she was a teen, Barbara was ready to leave behind certain traditional roles. When she learned her high school had a rule that prevented girls from participating in organized sports, she protested by becoming coach of the all-boys baseball team. As a senior at Brooklyn College in 1962, Barbara married Stewart Boxer. That same year she organized the tenants in her apartment building to persuade the landlord to make needed improvements. And she was sexually harassed by her economics professor. She didn't talk about the incident for thirty years, but the anger it caused would later help fuel her political energy.

After graduating from college, Boxer tried to get hired as a Wall Street stockbroker. But the firm she was employed by hired only men for those positions, so she was forced to take a job as a secretary. She passed the stockbrokers' exam, but had to move to another firm in order to work as a commissioned stockbroker. Three years later, she and her husband moved to San Francisco, where their son, Doug, was born, two months premature. The boy survived and two years later became an older brother to Nicole. The family then moved to the town of Greenbrae, north of San Francisco. There, Boxer organized the Education Corps of Marin County, a group aimed at reducing the high school dropout rate. She also helped start a women's political group and a day-care center.

In 1971, Boxer ran for a seat on the Marin County Board of Supervisors. She was surprised by the discouraging remarks from both men and women, who said she should be home taking care of her family. Despite a strong campaign, Boxer lost the election. Four years later, however, she won that seat. She served on the board from 1977 to 1983, while also becoming involved in several other political organizations. In 1980, she was the first woman ever elected president of the Marin County Board of Supervisors. In 1983, she was elected to the U.S. House of Representatives. As a freshman congresswoman, Boxer sent House Speaker Tip O'Neill a letter asking him to stop referring to his colleagues as "the men in Congress." He apologized for seeming to exclude the women. Boxer had set the tone that would become her trademark: polite but forceful. She fought for women's rights even within Congress itself, securing improved bathroom and exercise facilities for women inside the Capitol.

But it was Boxer's willingness to step into male-dominated arenas that won her recognition and popularity among voters. Angered by coffee pots that cost seven thousand dollars and other examples of wasteful military spending, Boxer introduced legislation that created more competition among defense contractors. As a result, American taxpayers saved more than a billion dollars by 1994. Boxer was named cochair of the Military Reform Caucus. She served on the Select Committee on Children, Youth, and Families; the Budget Committee; the Armed Services Committee; and the Government Operations Committee. In 1991, she authored the Violence Against Women Act, which helped fund rape prevention programs and women's shelters. And she watched on television, along with millions of other Americans, as the Senate Judiciary Committee conducted its confirmation hearings for the nomination of Clarence Thomas to the Supreme Court. During those hearings, Anita Hill, a former Thomas coworker, charged him with sexual harassment. To many women, the all-male committee seemed incapable of understanding the seriousness of the charges. The senators voted to confirm Thomas, who is now an associate justice on the Supreme Court. The decision sparked a nationwide outcry, especially among women. They entered and won elections in record numbers.

In June 1992, Boxer won the primary election for Alan Cranston's vacant Senate seat. Campaigning with San Francisco Mayor Dianne Feinstein, Boxer won the general election in November. (When Feinstein was elected to California's other Senate seat that same year, it marked the first time a state's two senators were both women.)

Declining an invitation to serve on the Judiciary Committee, Boxer joined the powerful Committee on Banking, Housing, and Urban Affairs. She has also served on numerous other committees and subcommittees. Boxer has pushed for tougher enforcement of immigration laws, while also trying to protect the human rights of illegal immigrants. She sponsored several parts of the 1994 crime bill, including increased penalties for arson. She supports a woman's right to choose an abortion and has introduced legislation that would provide more funding for the care of children.

Carol Moseley-Braun

First African-American
Woman in the Senate
1947–

*A*n unstoppable force came blasting out of Illinois and into the United States Senate in 1992. Her name was Carol Moseley-Braun, the first African-American woman to serve in the Senate. She had been angered by the treatment of Anita Hill during the Clarence Thomas confirmation hearings. What she saw on television was what millions of Americans saw: a Senate dominated by middle-aged-to-elderly white men. She believed that many Americans were not being adequately represented in Washington. Much to the surprise of her friends and colleagues, she decided to do something about it.

Carol Elizabeth Moseley was born on August 16, 1947, in Chicago, the oldest of four children. Her father, Joseph Moseley, was a policeman, and her mother, Edna Davie Moseley, was a medical technician. In 1963, Carol's parents divorced. She moved, with her mother and siblings, to her grandmother's house in a Chicago neighborhood known for its violent crime. During the next few years, Carol began to experience some of the injustice she would later work to eliminate. As a high school student, she staged a sit-in when she was denied service at a local restaurant because of her skin color. She visited an all-white beach, even though she expected the stones that were indeed thrown at her. She joined Martin Luther King Jr. in a civil rights march in Chicago.

In 1968, Carol entered the world of formal politics when she worked for Harold Washington, a state representative who would eventually become Chicago's first African-American mayor. The next year she graduated from the University of Illinois at Chicago, where she earned a bachelor's degree in political science, which she followed with a doctorate of law from the University of Chicago Law School. In 1973, she was hired as an assistant United States attorney in the U.S. District Court of Illinois. That same year she married Michael Braun, whom she had met in law school. Then in 1978, Moseley-Braun ran for a seat in the Illinois House of Representatives. She won the election and spent the next ten years learning the rules and players in the game of state politics. While in Springfield, Moseley-Braun supported gun control, welfare reform, and universal health care. She pushed for programs that aided women and minorities, and sponsored bills that would revamp the structure of Chicago's school councils. And she fought the death penalty. In 1980, she sued the Democratic Party over a redistricting plan she felt would hurt African-American and Hispanic representation on Chicago's South Side. Fighting against her fellow Democrats, she won the suit and the plan was dropped. In 1985, Moseley-Braun became the first woman and the first African-American to become an assistant majority leader in the state legislature. She divorced Michael Braun in 1986 (they have a son, Matthew).

Encouraged by Chicago mayor Harold Washington, Moseley-Braun ran, in 1987, for the post of Cook County recorder of deeds. When she took office as the first African-American ever elected to an executive position in the Cook County government, she assumed responsibility for three hundred employees and an $8 million budget. Four years later, the office had been completely modernized, reorganized, and nearly cleansed of corruption. Then, in 1991, Moseley-Braun shocked everyone who knew her by announcing that she would challenge Alan Dixon for his United States Senate seat. She had grown bored with her job as recorder of deeds. But a stronger catalyst was the frustration she felt as she watched the Anita Hill-Clarence Thomas hearings. "The Senate had exposed itself and demystified itself," said Moseley-Braun. "Most folks had thought of the U.S. Senate as this lofty body of great thinkers dealing with the issues of our time, and what they saw were some garden-variety politicians making bad speeches."

As she spoke out on numerous issues, Moseley-Braun's support grew rapidly. But she had no money, no organization, and very little of the political backing needed to get elected to Congress. Nevertheless, she won the Democratic primary in March 1992, then carried 53 percent of the vote in the general election in November. Perhaps most significant, Moseley-Braun did well among virtually every demographic group. She attracted votes from African-Americans, whites, women, men, young, and old.

After being sworn in as the first African-American woman in the Senate, Moseley-Braun was appointed to the Judiciary Committee and the Banking, Housing, and Urban Affairs Committee. She quickly established herself as a force to be reckoned with in the summer of 1993. The Senate was to vote on an amendment that would grant a federal patent on the insignia of the United Daughters of the Confederacy. The insignia included a Confederate flag, a symbol that, according to Moseley-Braun, gave honor to the former practice of slavery in the South. When a majority of the senators voted to approve the amendment, the freshman from Illinois single-handedly turned them around with a fiery speech from the Senate floor. Her colleagues agreed to vote again. This time they rejected the amendment.

Moseley-Braun has been a staunch advocate for schoolchildren. The Education Infrastructure Act, which she initiated and helped pass, channels federal resources to the renovation of elementary and secondary schools and libraries. She also coordinated Project Synergy, a program that helped Chicago students become familiar with computers and modems, which were donated by local businesses. She has fought for laws that benefit single parents, farmers, the disabled, and the poor. Moseley-Braun is on the Finance Committee and has also worked on the Special Committee on Aging.

Madeleine Albright

First Female
Secretary of State
1937–

*D*uring the 1940s, communism was spreading across eastern Europe. It crouched on the borders of Czechoslovakia, waiting for a chance to pounce. Meanwhile, within those borders, a young girl named Madeleine was growing up. The daughter of a diplomat, Madeleine traveled a great deal as the family moved from country to country. Then, in 1948, the Communists finally moved in and took control of the Czech government. Madeleine's father was charged with crimes against the state and sentenced to death. Nearly fifty years later, Madeleine would serve the United States of America as its representative to the United

Nations and then in the cabinet as secretary of state.

Madeleine Korbel was born on May 15, 1937, in Prague, the capital of Czechoslovakia. Her parents were Josef and Anna Korbel, and she had one sister, Anna, and one brother, John. Madeleine's father was a Czech diplomat. From the time Madeleine was born until the year the Korbels left Czechoslovakia, the family lived in Yugoslavia, England, Czechoslovakia, and Yugoslavia again. From a young age, Madeleine was comfortable interacting with visiting dignitaries and became fluent in English. Her father hired tutors to teach her at home, rather than send her to communist-run schools. When she was ten, Madeleine was enrolled in a school in Switzerland, where she learned French.

In 1948, Josef Korbel was sent to India as part of the U.N. Commission for India and Pakistan. Just weeks later Czechoslovakia was taken over by the communists. Korbel was sentenced to death for unspecified crimes. The following year, the family was granted asylum in the United States and settled in Colorado. Josef was hired as a professor of international relations by the University of Denver. He went on to write many books and was eventually named dean of the university's Graduate School of International Studies. By Madeleine's own account, her father was most responsible for her understanding of international political affairs.

Madeleine attended a small private high school, and after graduating in 1955, enrolled in Wellesley College in Massachusetts, where she majored in political science. She worked for Adlai Stevenson's presidential campaign in 1956, edited the college newspaper, and graduated with honors in 1959. Three days later, Madeleine married Joseph Albright and the newlyweds settled in Chicago, where Joseph worked as a reporter for the *Chicago Sun-Times*. Madeleine herself landed a job interview at the newspaper but was told by an editor that, because of potential conflicts of interest, no Chicago newspaper would ever hire the wife of a *Sun-Times* reporter. He further advised her to pursue some other career.

In 1961, Joseph was hired by *Newsday* in New York, and he and Madeleine moved to Long Island. Over the next six years, the Albrights had three daughters. Madeleine attended the graduate program in public law and government at Columbia University in New York City. In 1968, she received her master's degree and a certificate in Russian studies from Columbia. Meanwhile, her husband had been promoted to Washington bureau chief at *Newsday*, and the Albrights moved to the nation's capital. In 1972, Madeleine worked as a fund-raiser for Edmund Muskie's presidential campaign. Six years later, she joined the staff of the National Security Council, where she worked under Zbigniew Brzezinski, who had been one of her professors at Columbia. Brzezinski was now President Jimmy Carter's national security adviser. When Ronald Reagan was elected president in 1980, Albright temporarily left politics. She went to Georgetown University in Washington, where she had been appointed research professor of international affairs and director of the Women in Foreign Service Program. In 1981, she was awarded a Woodrow Wilson Fellowship at the Smithsonian Institution's Woodrow Wilson Center for Scholars. In 1983, she published *Poland: The Role of the Press in Political Change*. She also ended her marriage to Joseph Albright.

Madeleine worked for Walter Mondale's presidential campaign and Geraldine Ferraro's vice presidential campaign in 1984. In 1987, she was named senior foreign policy adviser to Michael Dukakis during his failed bid for the presidency. Two years later, she became president of the Center for National Policy. Madeleine Albright had become one of the nation's most respected and influential experts on foreign policy. She worked closely with Bill Clinton's top advisers after he was elected president in 1992. In December of that year, Clinton selected Albright as ambassador to the UN. She was unanimously approved by the Senate on January 27, 1993. As a key foreign policy adviser to the president, Albright often found herself commuting between Washington and the UN headquarters in New York City five times a week. She worked to ease conflicts all over the world, including those in eastern Europe, Africa, the former Soviet Union, southeast Asia, Central America, and the Caribbean.

Madeleine Albright was named secretary of state by Bill Clinton in 1996. She is the first woman ever to hold that post. She has written three books, speaks five languages, and has received countless awards.

Shortly after her appointment to the Cabinet, Albright learned that she is Jewish by birth, and that several members of her family were killed in the Holocaust by the Nazis. This discovery only strengthened her determination to help those abused by oppressive governments and war. She continues to work tirelessly to improve conditions for people everywhere.

Gro Harlem Brundtland

Norway's Champion
of the Environment
1939–

*I*n politics, the energy of youth is often perceived as an advantage. At the same time, nothing is more valuable than experience. Gro Harlem Brundtland has both. The first time she became Norway's prime minister, she was the youngest woman ever to take the reins of a modern government. She has now held the office on three separate occasions. She has the courage to make difficult economic decisions, as well as the sensitivity to care about the people who will be affected by her actions. And her passion for preserving the environment is an example of the long-term vision that has made Brundtland a true leader on the world stage.

Gro Harlem was born on April 20, 1939, in Oslo, the capital of Norway. She was one of four children born to Gudmund and Inga Harlem. Gudmund was the personal physician to several Labor Party prime ministers. Between 1955 and 1965, he also served as Norway's minister for social affairs and then minister of defense. When Gro was two, the family sneaked across the border to Sweden to escape the Nazi occupation of Norway. They remained in Stockholm while Gudmund served in Norway's anti-Nazi resistance movement. The Harlems returned to Norway in 1945.

Both of Gro's parents were political activists, and she became involved in a Labor Party youth group at age seven. When Gro was a student in senior secondary school, she worked on the executive committee of the students' socialist union. As a medical student at the University of Oslo, she served as vice chairman of the socialist students' association, a segment of the Labor Party. In 1960 Gro married Arne Olav Brundtland, a political science student. She graduated in 1963 with a doctor of medicine degree. Both Arne and Gro then traveled to the United States to do graduate work at Harvard University. Gro's studies at Harvard's School of Public Health inspired her later support of environmental issues. They returned to Oslo in 1965, and Gro became a consultant to the Ministry of Health and Social Affairs. Numerous other government positions involving health care services soon followed. In 1974, Prime Minister Trygve Bratteli appointed her minister of environmental affairs. The following year she was elected vice chairman of the Labor Party.

Brundtland supported the establishment of nature preserves and sought to protect the environment from Norway's offshore oil drilling industry in the North Sea. She worked to establish a nuclear weapon–free zone throughout all of Scandinavia. In 1977, she was elected to the Storting, which is Norway's parliament. As a member of the Storting, Brundtland was involved in committees on finance, foreign affairs, and the constitution. In October 1979, she resigned her cabinet post in order to devote more time to strengthening the Labor Party. Then, in January 1981, Prime Minister Odvar Nordli resigned. He offered his poor health as a reason, but many believed he was urged to quit by worried leaders of the weakening Labor Party. On February 3, the party's central committee unanimously elected Gro Harlem Brundtland Norway's twenty-second (and first woman) prime minister. In April 1981, she was also elected to the Labor Party's top post, uniting the positions of prime minister and party chairman.

Although Brundtland was popular, Norway's economic condition continued to decline. As the elections grew nearer, the Conservative Party's platform of lower taxes and reduced spending looked more and more appealing to voters. On September 14, 1981, the Conservatives took about 55 percent of the vote. Thirty days later, Kare Willoch took over as prime minister. Brundtland's term in office had lasted a little over eight months. However, she remained in the Storting. In 1984, she became chairman of the United Nations World Commission on Environment and Development. The group studied environmental problems in several countries and issued findings and recommendations. Brundtland has consistently called for industrialized nations to find ways to continue economic growth while using less energy. In this way, she explains, there will be sufficient natural resources left for developing countries.

Brundtland was again chosen as prime minister when the Labor Party staged a comeback in 1986. She remained in office until 1989, then returned again in 1990 and served until 1998, when she was appointed to a five-year term as head of the World Health Organization, a position that allowed her to combine her interest and skills in medicine and public health with her talents and abilities in politics.

Gro Harlem and Arne Olav Brundtland live in Oslo, where they have raised four children. She remains a strong supporter of programs to benefit women and the environment. Her husband is a leading member of the opposition Conservative Party. Thus, even in her home, Gro Harlem has round-the-clock practice in the art of dealing diplomatically with people of different viewpoints.

Patricia Schroeder

Twelve-Term
Congresswoman
1940–

In 1972, James Schroeder was a rookie campaign manager eager to get involved in the race for Congress in Colorado. The Republican candidate, incumbent Mike McKevitt, was widely held as a shoo-in for reelection. The Democratic candidate, if Schroeder could find one, would almost certainly be led to slaughter. To enter the race would be political suicide. Sure enough, the people on his list of possibilities turned him down, one after another. Schroeder needed to find someone, and he was getting desperate. But who would be crazy enough to run against McKevitt?

Patricia Scott was born on July 30, 1940, in Portland, Oregon, the daughter of Lee and Bernice Scott. Pat attended Portland public schools through high school, then enrolled in the University of Minnesota in Minneapolis. She graduated in three years, magna cum laude and Phi Beta Kappa. She then headed to Harvard Law School, where she received a doctorate of law in 1964. At Harvard, she met James Schroeder, and they were married on August 18, 1962. They enjoyed working together and both planned to go into law. But James also had a strong interest in politics.

After graduation, the Schroeders moved to Denver, Colorado, where Pat landed a job as field attorney for the National Labor Relations Board. She was responsible for the Colorado-Utah-Wyoming region. In June 1966, the Schroeders had their first child, Scott William. In 1968, Pat worked as a precinct committeewoman for the Democratic Party, then returned to private law practice the following year. She also worked as a lecturer and instructor at several colleges over the next four years. A second child, Jamie Christine, was born in 1970. After the baby, Pat served as legal counsel for the Colorado branch of Planned Parenthood. She was also employed by the Colorado Department of Personnel.

In 1972, Schroeder was convinced by her husband to enter the race for the U.S. House of Representatives. She filed her candidacy in May of that year but was so sure she would lose that she kept working at her jobs right up until Election Day. But James had organized a masterful campaign, orchestrating a large team of grassroots volunteers and sharply focused messages. Meanwhile, Pat came out strongly against the Vietnam War. She called for improvements in education, health services, child care, and environmental programs. Endorsed by local Democratic groups and organized labor, Pat won the primary in September, then took the election from McKevitt in November. Pat Schroeder was off to Washington as the representative from Colorado's First Congressional District.

Representative Pat Schroeder is shown here with First Lady Hillary Rodham Clinton and Representative Olympia Snowe at the 1993 Congressional Caucus for Women's Issues.

On Capitol Hill, her welcome from male colleagues was not generally warm. When one representative asked Pat how she could be the mother of two children and a member of Congress at the same time, she replied, "I have a brain and a uterus, and I use them both." Schroeder then pushed her way onto the powerful Armed Services Committee, a group with a long and friendly relationship with the Pentagon and the U.S. military. She began speaking out against excessive military spending and waste, launching a relentless attack against both the committee and the Pentagon. And she backed up her words with action, voting against ever bigger and more deadly weapons systems she believed were unnecessary. At the same time, she pushed for school lunch subsidies, Social Security increases, better emergency medical services, more effective aid for child abuse victims, and a heightened awareness of environmental issues.

In 1974, Schroeder ran unopposed in the primary, then defeated her

Republican opponent by taking 58 percent of the vote. Two years later, she grabbed 54 percent in winning a third term. She went on to serve twelve terms in the House of Representatives. Throughout her career, Schroeder fought for women's rights. She was chair of the National Task Force on Equal Rights for Women. She pushed to pass Title IX of the 1972 Educational Amendments. (Title IX says that no person may be excluded on the basis of sex from participating in federally funded education programs.) And she campaigned long and hard in favor of the ERA, an amendment to the United States Constitution intended to ensure equal rights for women.

In addition, she worked for improved child-care programs, increased funding for education, and changes that would encourage higher voter registration. In 1984, Schroeder served as cochair of Gary Hart's presidential campaign. She voted to allow military women to fly combat missions. And she was a tireless opponent of sexual harassment in the armed forces.

After twenty-four years of long workdays and frequent travel between Washington and Colorado, Schroeder decided she'd done enough. She did not run for reelection in 1996.

Mary Robinson

One of Ireland's
Bright Lights
1944–

*M*ary Robinson has deep respect for all people, but she has a special sensitivity to the underdog. She has voiced support for, and has been active in reaching out to, unwed mothers, minorities, the impoverished, gays and lesbians, and the disabled, among others. That should come as no surprise. Robinson knows exactly what it feels like to have people expect you to lose. She was a 100-to-1 underdog in her race for Ireland's presidency.

Mary Bourke was born May 21, 1944, in Ballina, County Mayo, Ireland. Her parents were both Catholic, and both physicians, though her mother retired in order to raise her five children. All five of those children—Mary and four brothers—graduated from Trinity College in Dublin. In 1967, Mary earned a bachelor of arts degree in French, and she then went on to receive a law degree. Her academic performance was exceptional, and she received a scholarship to do graduate work in law at Harvard University. She returned to Ireland at age twenty-five to become the youngest law professor in the long history of Trinity College.

Robinson was elected to the upper house (senate) of the Irish parliament in 1969 and served there for twenty years as a member of the Labour Party. When she began her tenure in the senate, strict laws were in place prohibiting divorce and homosexuality. The purchase of contraceptives was impossible without a doctor's prescription. Robinson was instrumental in changing those barriers and worked successfully to help women gain equal pay. She was also active in trying to improve relations between Catholics and Protestants. In a true case of practicing what she preaches, Robinson is married to a Trinity College alumnus, Nicholas Robinson, who is Protestant. They have three children.

Nominated by her party to run for president in 1990, Robinson was a long shot to win. Her opponents were conservative men backed by Ireland's two largest political parties, and her views often flew in the face of the views of the Catholic Church, which is a dominant force in Ireland. But Robinson wouldn't be denied, campaigning far into the night and from one end of Ireland to the other. She was sworn in to her seven-year term on December 3, 1990. The victory was the first by an Irish woman.

The office of president is mostly symbolic in Ireland; it is the prime minister who holds the political power. The president cannot even deliver a speech or leave the country without permission. But Robinson used those restrictions to her advantage. Rather than reaching large groups on a broad level, she found ways to touch individual lives more deeply, and more permanently. As the president herself described it, "It's important to listen. . . . A phrase you use is appropriate only when you've been listening, in touch with the small print of people's lives."

Robinson announced in 1997 that she did not intend to seek another term. While in office, she kept a light burning constantly in a second-floor window of the presidential mansion. The light was put there as a symbol to Irish people, wherever they are in the world, that they are remembered, and that they will always have a connection to their homeland.

Wilma Mankiller

First Woman Chief of
the Cherokee Nation
1945–

*I*n 1979, Wilma Man-killer was near death after a terrible car crash. She would endure seventeen difficult operations before her ordeal was over. Just six years later, Mankiller would become the first woman chief in the long and proud history of the Cher-okee tribe.

Wilma Pearl Mankiller was born in Stillwell, Oklahoma, on November 18, 1945. When Wilma was eleven, the Mankiller farm went bankrupt, and the United States Bureau of Indian Affairs sent the family to San Francisco. The move was part of a nationwide program to relocate Native Americans from rural to urban areas. Like many Native Americans in similar situations, the

Mankillers had trouble adjusting to their new life in a low-income housing project. But they worked hard to make the best of it.

Eventually, Wilma graduated from high school, got married, and began to raise a family. But her roots haunted her, and she never felt at home or content in the lifestyle that had been forced upon her. Then, in 1969, a group called the American Indian Movement (AIM) took over Alcatraz Island, near San Francisco. Alcatraz had once been Indian territory. In later years it became a military site and then a federal prison. AIM claimed that the land belonged to them, and they refused to leave. The occupation lasted eighteen months. During that time, Wilma raised money to support AIM. Although the attempt to reclaim Alcatraz was doomed to failure, Mankiller had gotten back in touch with her people and her heritage. She was destined to do great things for Native Americans, and the process had begun.

Mankiller studied sociology at San Francisco State University and continued to advocate for property and treaty rights for several Indian tribes. In 1977, she returned to Oklahoma and worked as a community organizer for the Cherokee Nation, the second-largest tribe in the United States. She fought to improve health care, housing, education, and employment for Native Americans.

Following the near-fatal accident in 1979, Mankiller resumed her community development projects, many of which would serve as models for other tribes. In 1983, she was chosen by Ross Swimmer, the tribe's chief, to serve as deputy chief of the Cherokee Nation. When Swimmer resigned in 1985 to head the Bureau of Indian Affairs, Mankiller succeeded him as chief.

Mankiller constantly pushed for reforms that would help the tribe. She founded the Cherokee Nation's first chamber of commerce, which made an important connection between tribal businesses and American society at large. She worked closely with the Environmental Protection Agency whenever a project threatened Cherokee land. And she established the Institute for Cherokee Literacy, believing that education was the most important factor in the Native American's quest for opportunity and freedom. Mankiller was reelected in 1987, and then again in 1991. During her time as chief, the tribe's membership increased from 55,000 to 156,000.

In 1994, Mankiller chose not to run for re-election. She continues to work for the advancement of the Cherokee Nation in the areas of business, education, health care, and housing. At the same time, she seeks to preserve the culture of her tribe for future generations—a culture that was taken away from her throughout much of her childhood.

Christie Todd Whitman

First Woman Governor
of New Jersey
1946–

In 1990, Christine Todd Whitman ran against a very popular Democrat. He was considered by many to be unbeatable in the Senate, and perhaps even presidential material. Whitman lost the election by just a few thousand votes and immediately became a national figure. By 1994, she was the only woman occupying a governor's office, and was herself being hailed as a potential candidate for either vice president or president.

Christine Temple Todd was born in New York City on September 26, 1946. The youngest of Webster and Eleanor Todd's four children, Christie spent most of her first thirteen years on the family estate, Pontefract, in rural New

Jersey. The estate, also a working farm, proved to be the perfect setting for Christie, who enjoyed fishing, riding horses, and exploring the nearby woods and fields. But while she climbed trees and chased cows and chickens, a family political tradition was also taking root in Christie's mind and heart. Her father was Republican state chairman in New Jersey during the 1960s and 1970s. Her mother was vice chair of the Republican National Committee and chaired the New Jersey state finance committee of George Bush's campaign for the presidential nomination in 1980. During the 1950s, she herself had often been described as a prime candidate to become New Jersey's first woman governor. In addition, Christie's two brothers and her sister have all served as elected or appointed officials on the local, state, and federal levels.

When Christie turned fourteen, she went off to the Foxcroft School in Middleburg, Virginia. Though away from her family, Christie continued to be absorbed in their political activities. She frequently engaged in debates with her father, counted ballots with her mother, and attended numerous speeches and conventions. On separate occasions, she met President Dwight Eisenhower and Vice President Richard Nixon.

In 1968, Christie graduated from Wheaton College with a bachelor of arts degree in government. She then went to work for the Republican National Committee. One of her tasks was to improve relations between the party and groups such as senior citizens, minorities, the handicapped, and students. Christie also worked for the Office of Economic Opportunity, and in the early 1970s, on President Nixon's reelection campaign. On April 20, 1974, Christie married John Russell Whitman, the son of a New York judge and the grandson of a former New York governor.

Christie was elected in 1982 to the Somerset County Board of Chosen Freeholders ("freeholder" is a term used in New Jersey to indicate a county official). She served on the board for more than five years. During that time, she oversaw the construction of a new courthouse, completed on schedule and under budget, and helped establish the county's first homeless shelter. In 1988, Governor Tom Kean chose Whitman to serve as president of the New Jersey Board of Public Utilities. After resigning that position two years later, Whitman shocked everyone by entering the race for the United States Senate. At the time, her opponent, incumbent Bill Bradley, enjoyed 98 percent name recognition among New Jersey voters. Whitman's was 10 percent. No one thought she had much chance to win, especially given her short supply of funds. After spending just $1 million on her campaign (Bradley spent $12 million), Whitman gathered 49 percent of the vote, losing the election but giving Bradley the scare of his political life.

Whitman maintained her newly acquired popularity by writing newspaper columns, hosting a radio talk show, and campaigning for various Republican candidates around the state. In 1993, she launched her candidacy for the governor's office. After winning the nomination of the Republican Party, Whitman campaigned vigorously against Governor Jim Florio. The incumbent was experienced but very unpopular, especially because he had promised not to raise taxes, and then did. Toward the end of the campaign, Whitman capitalized on her opponent's weakness by pledging to cut New Jersey income taxes by 30 percent over three years. On November 2, Whitman and Florio split the 2.5 million votes cast, but not perfectly: Whitman won by about 26,000 ballots.

On the day she was sworn in, Governor Whitman proposed a 5 percent tax cut for individuals and businesses. Six months later, she reduced the tax by another 10 percent. Meanwhile, she had already erased the $2 billion budget deficit inherited from the Florio administration. During her first three years in office, Whitman continued to implement her campaign slogan "For the people." By the end of her first term, she had lowered state income tax by the promised 30 percent. And political experts around the country began mentioning Whitman as a possible candidate for the White House.

In her 1997 race for reelection, Whitman did not pull off the landslide victory many had expected against her Democratic challenger, James McGreevey. In fact, the race turned out to be one of the closest in state history, with Whitman winning by a margin of 22,000 votes out of 2.37 million cast. High property taxes and auto insurance rates were the reasons most often cited for voters' unhappiness with the governor. In her victory speech, Whitman promised to work harder on those issues and to become a stronger advocate for the state's middle class.

Hanna Suchocka

Strong, Resilient,
Courageous
1946–

Hanna Suchocka was a fine product of her upbringing. She was responsible and a high achiever. She compiled a perfect attendance record in school and studied foreign languages, literature, and music, as all Polish girls were supposed to do. Poland during the 1940s and 1950s was firmly within the brutal grip of communist dictators. The hope of a democratic election existed only in the dreams of the most optimistic citizens. The idea of a woman winning those elections seemed impossible. If young Hanna ever thought about becoming the political leader of Poland, she surely kept the notion to herself.

Hanna Suchocka was born April 3, 1946, in Pleszew, Poland. Her parents owned the pharmacy in town, and the family lived in a second-story apartment above the store. She went to church regularly and dreamed of traveling around Europe. Although her parents hoped she would become a pharmacist, Hanna went on to study law at Poznan University, where her grandfather had been a lecturer years before. After graduating in 1968, Hanna accepted a teaching position in the law department at Poznan. However, all faculty members were expected to join the Communist Party. Hanna criticized the party's atheistic teachings and refused to join. The following year, the school did not renew her teaching contract. She then joined the Democratic Party and took a job with the Institute of Small Arts and Crafts. In 1973, Poznan University rehired Hanna. By then, she was working on her doctorate in constitutional law.

In 1980, Suchocka was elected to the Sejm, the lower house of Poland's parliament. Later that year, Lech Walesa founded a labor movement called Solidarity, which achieved worldwide attention. Suchocka joined Solidarity and was asked to be one of its legal advisers. On December 13, 1981, the country's leader, General Wojciech Jaruzelski, declared martial law. Suchocka was one of only a handful of legislators who voted against the decision. Three years later, the government outlawed Solidarity, and Suchocka again refused to vote in agreement. She was soon expelled from the legislature.

When the Communist government fell in Poland in 1989, Suchocka returned to the Sejm. She has earned a reputation as a conservative legislator, voting against legalized abortion, sex education in school, and other similar issues. In 1991, Suchocka won reelection as a member of the Democratic Union, a party she helped establish. One of the aims of the party is to foster the growth of capitalism in Poland.

In 1991 elections, the first completely democratic elections in Poland since the end of Communist rule, Lech Walesa was chosen president. The following year, an election for prime minister was held. No clear winner emerged, so a shaky collection of representatives from twenty-nine different parties ruled. The government, led by Polish Peasants Party leader Waldemar Pawlak, crumbled after five weeks. Then someone in the Sejm suggested Hanna Suchocka become a candidate for prime minister. After the lawmakers managed to get past the idea of a woman leading the country, no one could think of a better candidate. Informed of their decision, Suchocka refused to even consider the possibility, claiming she was not qualified for such a job. However, she was soon persuaded to change her mind and by July 1992 had won the support of seven different parties.

On July 8, Suchocka was nominated for the office of prime minister by President Walesa. Two days later she was confirmed by a 233–61 vote in the Sejm. Suchocka immediately set out to bring the various parties together, to finally distinguish between the powers of the president and the prime minister, and to help Poland move smoothly from communism to capitalism. But widespread labor strikes had to be dealt with first. Workers in the automobile and mining industries were demanding higher wages. When Suchocka took a firm stand against the strikers, they backed down and returned to work. Productivity in the factories quickly improved and inflation declined dramatically. But wages also dropped, and many workers lost their jobs.

The transition from communism to capitalism required many people in Poland to make sacrifices. Under communism, workers had had little freedom but could count on a certain level of financial security. Capitalism offers a wide-open market in which people are free to take risks and possibly make a fortune. But it does not offer protection for those who fail, and success is often a long-term process. Such a change from one system to another takes time, and courage. Suchocka's government was caught in that moment in time when many people were not yet willing to completely let go of the old ways. In September 1993, elections were held and Suchocka's Democratic Union party barely collected 10 percent of the vote. On October 26, she stepped down as prime minister and was replaced by Waldemar Pawlak.

Suchocka remains a member of the Sejm. She speaks Polish, German, English, and French, and enjoys playing the piano and attending the opera.

Tansu Çiller

First Woman Prime
Minister of Turkey
1946–

Tansu Çiller entered politics in 1991. Two years later she was prime minister of Turkey, the first woman to lead that nation. The accomplishment cannot be overestimated. Turkey is a land in which only affluent women have opportunities equal to those of men. Çiller is the third woman to head a predominantly Muslim country (after Benazir Bhutto of Pakistan and Khaleda Zia of Bangladesh) but is the first to do so without the benefit of a family that is political on a national level. She took office at a critical time in Turkey's development as a modern nation.

Tansu Çiller was born in 1946 in Istanbul, Turkey. Her father was a provincial governor, and the family was quite wealthy. Tansu attended the American College for Girls in Istanbul, then got married at age seventeen. (In a highly unusual gesture, especially in Turkey, her husband Ozer took her last name.) Tansu graduated from Robert College in 1967 with a degree in economics. Traveling to the United States with her husband, she earned a master's degree in economics from the University of New Hampshire and a doctorate in economics from the University of Connecticut. She completed postdoctoral studies at Yale, then taught for several years at Franklin and Marshall College in Pennsylvania.

In 1974, the Çillers returned to Turkey, where Tansu was hired to teach economics at Robert College, now called Bosporus University. In 1983, she was promoted to full professor, the youngest person ever to reach that status in Turkey. Çiller also worked as a consultant to the World Bank's Chamber of Industry and Trade Board and was an adviser to the Istanbul Metropolitan Municipality. In 1989 she wrote a report criticizing the way the president and his Motherland Party were handling Turkey's national debt. As a result, Çiller was invited to join the ranks of the True Path Party. She was quickly elevated to the party's executive board and served as its deputy chairperson.

When the True Path Party defeated the Motherland Party in the 1991 elections, Süleyman Demirel was named prime minister. Demirel appointed Çiller to his cabinet as minister of state for the economy. She was also elected a deputy of the General Assembly. Çiller immediately proposed turning many of Turkey's state-owned monopolies into private businesses.

Within a short time, Çiller was criticized for failing to bring down interest rates and for her inability to privatize the state-owned monopolies. When President Turgut Ozal died in April 1993, Demirel was elected to fill the vacancy, which left the prime minister's office up for grabs. Çiller resigned her cabinet position in order to qualify as a candidate. The Turkish media believed

Çiller did not have enough party support to win. In fact, several party leaders were critical of Çiller and doubtful of her chances for success. But she conducted a solid campaign, emphasizing stronger alliances with the West and a more modern Turkey. On the second ballot, held June 13, 1993, she captured 933 of 1,169 delegate votes. Her victory brought enthusiastic celebrations: the people believed that welcome change was on the way.

Prime Minister Çiller ran into trouble almost immediately. Her party had twenty cabinet members in place; she fired seventeen of them. She was the only economist among the new cabinet members she appointed, a move perceived as her attempt to gain complete control. But she quickly got the legislature to pass dramatic reforms, including some concerning the budget and the sale of the hated state-owned monopolies.

In the streets, a different kind of problem was boiling over. Members of the Kurdish Workers' Party were engaging in terrorist activities. The Kurds consider themselves a persecuted minority in Turkey and claim these sometimes violent activities are a way of fighting back against the repressive government. Çiller did not see it that way and announced she would protect citizens against the actions of Kurdish guerrillas. She also got heavily involved in the conflict between the Azerbaijanis and their enemies, the Armenians. And in 1994, she traveled to Sarajevo with Benazir Bhutto to try to halt the civil war between Bosnia's Muslims and Serbs.

Çiller's popularity dropped in 1994 as the economy continued to stumble. Yet the True Path Party won a plurality of the vote in March elections. (When there are two candidates or parties in an election, the winner must get more than half the votes. When there are three or more candidates or parties running, the winner is the one who gets a "plurality"—or simply more than any other.) At the same time, the Islamic Welfare Party also won several important elections that year. Islamic Welfare called for cutting some ties to the West, including membership in NATO (North Atlantic Treaty Organization), and for reestablishing traditional Islamic social laws. Çiller saw these changes as obstacles to a truly modern Turkey.

In the December 1995 election, the Islamic Welfare Party collected 158 votes, while Çiller's True Path Party won 113. The two parties then formed an unexpected partnership. As a result, Necmettin Erbakan became head of the first Islamist-majority coalition government since Turkey became a secular state in 1923. Çiller became deputy prime minister and foreign minister. Their agreement called for Erbakan to serve as prime minister for two years, then hand the job back to Çiller and her conservative, nonreligious True Path Party. By June 1997, Erbakan had angered too many of his opponents, including the military, with his attempts to turn Turkey into an Islamic society. He resigned under pressure, hoping Çiller would be named prime minister (their alliance would have kept him in the power loop). But Çiller, too, was hounded from office by allegations of corruption, drug smuggling, and even spying for the U.S. Central Intelligence Agency. But she remained head of the True Path Party.

Hillary Rodham Clinton

The Most Influential
First Lady
1947–

Hillary Clinton has been the most active in a series of increasingly prominent First Ladies. Consider that Martha Washington didn't even attend George's inauguration, and it's easy to see the dramatic change that has taken place in the role of president's wife. Yes, Edith Wilson was nearly running the country in 1920, but her husband had suffered a stroke. Yes, Nancy Reagan attended cabinet meetings, but her aim was to assist the president. Hillary Clinton has skills and experience unmatched by her predecessors. Many political experts believe her career path could have led her to the Supreme Court, Congress, or the presidency.

Hillary Victoria Rodham was born on October 26, 1947, in Chicago, Illinois. Her parents were Hugh and Dorothy (Howell) Rodham. Hugh owned his own drapery business. Dorothy stayed at home to raise Hillary, Hugh Jr., and Anthony. She also took courses at local colleges, a curious activity for a mother in the 1950s. Traditional values were emphasized by both parents: loyalty, respect, hard work, church, school, sports. Young Hillary competed with her brothers and friends in every way. She could hit a curveball, throw a mean punch, and bake cookies. She won every Girl Scout badge and earned honors in school. In a neighborhood of fifty kids, Hillary was the leader. She was focused, goal-oriented, and had a natural need to help others.

When Hillary was fourteen, President John F. Kennedy called for America to reach the moon by 1970. Hillary wrote a letter to NASA, asking how she could become an astronaut. They responded that NASA did not accept girls as astronauts. Undiscouraged, Hillary continued to pursue academic success at Maine South High School. She was elected vice president of her junior class and was a member of the student council and the National Honor Society. After graduation, she enrolled in Wellesley College in Massachusetts.

Hillary had been exposed to a variety of political viewpoints by then, but her parents were Republican, and so was she. Then, in 1968, she went to Chicago to attend the Democratic National Convention. There, she saw protesters being beaten by police. The war in Vietnam was raging. Hillary's political views changed, and she went to work for Eugene McCarthy, a Democrat running for president. But Republican candidate Richard Nixon was elected. In 1969, she enrolled in the law school at Yale University. While at Yale she worked on Senator Walter Mondale's congressional subcommittee studying the living conditions of migrant workers. She volunteered at New Haven Hospital, assisting doctors on cases of child abuse. She became an editor of the *Yale Review of Law and Social Action*. And she met Bill Clinton.

Bill was smart, sensitive, and charming. Hillary was intellectual, practical, and focused. Both wanted to change the world, or at least part of it, and they made a perfect team. They worked on George McGovern's presidential campaign in 1972. A year later, they graduated from Yale. He returned to Arkansas to teach law at the University of Arkansas at Fayetteville. She traveled the country for what is now known as the Children's Defense Fund (CDF). Then, in January 1974, both were offered positions by the House of Representatives' Judiciary Committee, which was looking for young lawyers to help prepare impeachment proceedings against President Nixon, who was caught in the Watergate scandal. Bill turned the offer down. Hillary jumped at it.

For the next seven months, Hillary listened to tapes, researched the law, and helped establish legal procedures for impeaching the president. When Nixon resigned on August 9, Hillary found herself with several options. She could take a job with a law firm in New York or Washington, or she could return to the CDF. Instead, she was hired as an assistant professor of law at the University of Arkansas at Fayetteville. Bill was teaching also and launching his own campaign for Congress. He lost a close election. In October 1975, Bill and Hillary were married, and one year later he was elected attorney general of Arkansas. In 1977, Hillary was hired by the Rose Law Firm, the most prestigious in the state. The following year, Bill decided to run for governor, and Hillary, who had kept her last name, became a focus of his campaign. Hillary Rodham's feminist views contrasted sharply with those of many voters in rural Arkansas. Nevertheless, in November 1978, at age thirty-two, Bill Clinton was elected as the youngest governor in the nation. Two years later, he lost his bid for reelection, and Hillary gave birth to Chelsea. In January 1983, Bill was back in the governor's office, where he would remain until becoming president ten years later.

Hillary Rodham Clinton addresses a crowd attending an election rally for her husband, Bill Clinton, outside the statehouse in Providence, Rhode Island, during the 1992 campaign.

Throughout his career in Arkansas and Washington, Bill Clinton has pushed for reforms in health care, education, and child care. Hillary has worked closely with him and has often been the driving force behind those efforts. In 1993, the new president named Hillary chair of the Task Force on National Health Care Reform. The program never made it through Congress, and negative reactions to it can still be heard. In fact, Hillary has withstood a constant storm of criticism, mostly from those who believe she has acquired too much influence on national policy. Also, investigations into the Clintons' investment activities in Arkansas stalked the First Couple during their two terms in the White House. Through all the successes and controversies, Hillary has continued to do what she believes is right. Her response to her critics can be summed up in a speech she gave shortly after the death of her father in 1994. What we need as a nation, she said, "is a new politics of meaning . . . , of individual responsibility and caring . . . , a new definition of society which answers the unanswerable questions . . . as to how we can have a society that fills us up again and makes us feel that we are part of something bigger than ourselves." Hillary Rodham Clinton has long worked to help create such a society.

Olympia Snowe

Maverick Senator
from Maine
1947–

When Olympia Snowe was eight years old, her mother died of cancer. One year later, her father died of heart disease. When she was twenty-six, her husband was killed in a car accident. Look at Olympia Snowe today, and it might be hard to understand how this elegant woman ever got through to the voters of Maine's rugged northern districts, a land of potato farms and factories, forests and paper mills. But the people of Maine tend to favor candidates who are strong and independent, and who do what's right, not what's popular. Olympia Snowe had to find her strength and independence early in life. And she's worked hard ever since to fight for what she believes is right, even if it doesn't reflect popular opinion.

Olympia Jean Bouchles was born February 21, 1947, in Augusta, Maine. Her father, George John Bouchles, was a cook who had come to the United States from Mytilene, Greece. Her mother, Georgia Goranites Bouchles, was the daughter of Greek immigrants from Sparta. After her father died, Olympia was separated from her only sibling. She went to Auburn, Maine, to live with an aunt, uncle, and five cousins, while her brother was raised by another relative. In 1962, she entered Edward Little High School in Auburn. Within a year, her uncle died, and Olympia saw what a widowed textile-mill employee, working the night shift, had to go through to raise six children by herself. The lessons were tough, and Olympia never forgot what she learned.

After high school, Olympia went to the University of Maine at Orono, where she earned a bachelor's degree in political science in 1969. That same year she married a businessman named Peter Trafton Snowe, a Republican, who had become the youngest member of the state legislature in 1967. In 1970, Olympia went to work for the Auburn Board of Voter Registration. Two years later she was employed in the district office of United States congressman William Cohen.

In April 1973, Peter Snowe was killed in an accident while driving home from his office in Augusta. Later that year, Olympia was elected to the state house of representatives to fill her husband's vacant congressional seat. She had enjoyed working behind the scenes, but her passion for politics inspired her to seek reelection in 1974. She won the election and was an alternate delegate to the 1976 Republican National Convention. Snowe also chaired the Joint Standing Committee on Health and Institutional Services, where she established herself as a strong advocate of health care reform. When Cohen left office to run for the Senate in 1978, Snowe got the Republican nomination for his vacant seat in the U.S. House of Representatives. She campaigned

Senator Olympia Snowe poses here with some of her Maine constituents.

extensively across her district and won the election by ten percentage points. At thirty-one, Snowe was the youngest Republican woman and the first Greek-American woman ever elected to Congress. She was reelected in 1980 by a 79 to 21 percent margin. She went on to win the next four elections, never getting less than two-thirds of the vote.

Snowe cochaired, with Patricia Schroeder of Colorado, the Congressional Caucus for Women's Issues. From that base, she began pushing for legislation that would eliminate sex discrimination in insurance and pension laws and would benefit housewives and parents who pay for day care. She called for protection of social programs, cuts in defense spending, increased funding for energy conservation programs, and energy assistance to low-income households. In 1988, Snowe sponsored a bill that would increase the government's role in providing child-care services. The following year, she and Schroeder introduced legislation to establish five research centers that would study new methods of birth control, as well as treatments for infertility. Meanwhile, she maintained a good working relationship with Republican Party leaders, including President Ronald Reagan, who often disagreed with her policies.

The recession of the late 1980s hit hard in Maine, where Snowe's district lost forty thousand jobs. She was also hurt by budget cuts and tax increases implemented by John McKernan Jr., the governor of Maine—and Snowe's husband since 1989. She won the 1990 election with just 51 percent of the vote. In 1992, she defeated the same opponent, Patrick McGowan, by a 49 to 42 percent margin (a third candidate, Jonathan Carter, helped Snowe by taking votes away from McGowan). During her eighth term in the House, Snowe was a member of the Budget Committee and supported a constitutional amendment requiring a balanced federal budget. As a member of the Select Committee on Aging, she also pushed for more research on diseases among the elderly.

In 1994, Senate majority leader George Mitchell of Maine announced his retirement. Snowe won the election for his seat, gathering 60 percent of the vote. In the Senate, Snowe has continued to fight for the causes she believes in, including a balanced budget and more help for people who need it. Those causes sometimes call for more spending, sometimes less. Olympia Snowe doesn't follow formulas or party lines, and doesn't act according to what's popular. She follows her heart, and looks to do what's right—for her constituents in Maine, and for the United States as a nation.

Kim Campbell

First Woman Prime
Minister of Canada
1947–

Canada is the second-largest country in the world. With fewer people than the state of California, it is also one of the least densely populated. It is a confederation of many different groups of people, separated geographically and, in many ways, culturally. Even twenty years ago—before the age of fax machines, computers, and cell phones—it would have been an enormous challenge for a female candidate to convince enough voters to support a woman for prime minister. But in 1993, time, chance, and skill all came together.

Avril Phaedra Douglas Campbell was born on March 10, 1947, in Port Alberni, British Columbia. Her parents were George and Phyllis (Cook)

Campbell, both war veterans. Her sister, Alix, was born in 1945. After the war, George finished his studies and set up a law practice. Phyllis worked at various jobs and studied at the Vancouver School of Art. Avril and Alix were often cared for by their maternal grandmother, who returned to teaching at age sixty. She was a loving, adventurous person, and a role model for both girls. At the same time, Phyllis instilled in her daughters the importance of poetry, language, and education. They were given ballet and piano lessons and taught that women could do anything. In this setting, Avril developed her sense of humor, love of theatrics, independence, and ambition.

In 1957, Avril was chosen to appear as a regular on a children's television show. She interviewed guests and led panel discussions. In the process, she grew comfortable with a medium that would prove to be extremely important in her future career. That winter, her mother suffered a devastating fall in which she broke her hip. She never fully recovered from the mishap, and her marriage, which was already shaky, fell apart. Two years later, Phyllis and her husband separated, and George was left to care for his daughters. Around the same time, Avril changed her name and began calling herself Kim.

Kim Campbell attended St. Anne's Academy in Victoria, then went off to Prince of Wales Secondary School in Vancouver for ninth grade. In her senior year, she was elected student council president, the first girl to be so honored in the school's history. She was also class valedictorian. In the fall of 1964, she enrolled in the University of British Columbia as a political science major. As a freshman, she became the first woman elected president of UBC's Frosh Council, a political organization for first-year students. During this time, she began forming opinions about world politics. Among other things, she developed a strong dislike for communism. She was also affected by the women's movement. During her junior year, she met Nathan Divinsky, a math professor, who would become her first husband. After graduating with honors in

1970, Kim went to England for a year of graduate work at the London School of Economics and Political Science. There she studied the goals and failures of communist and noncommunist leaders. Also around this time, Kim was reunited with her mother, whom she hadn't seen in ten years. (Her parents had eventually divorced and both had remarried.)

After a three-month study trip to the Soviet Union, Kim married Nathan Divinsky. For the next five years, she taught at UBC. In 1980, she was elected to the Vancouver School Board, then entered UBC's law school. During the next three years, her marriage to Nathan ended and she became an attorney. Then, in the summer of 1985, Campbell was offered the position of executive director in the office of British Columbia premier Bill Bennett. A year later, Bennett stepped down, and Campbell ran, unsuccessfully, to replace him.

The next year, Campbell married Howard Eddy, an attorney. In November, she was elected to the British Columbia provincial legislature, where she served until 1988. That year, Campbell campaigned as a Progressive Conservative Party candidate and was elected to Canada's House of Commons. In January 1989, she was appointed minister of Indian affairs and northern development by Prime Minister Brian Mulroney. The following year, Mulroney named her minister of justice, and three years later, minister of defense and minister of veterans' affairs. Then, on February 24, 1993, with the Conservative Party struggling to hold onto power, Mulroney announced he was stepping down as prime minister. On June 13, 1993, Kim Campbell was elected leader of the Progressive Conservative Party. On June 25, she was sworn in as Canada's first woman prime minister.

Throughout her political career, Kim Campbell worked to bring unity to a large and often divided nation. She supported tougher gun control legislation, a woman's right to a safe and legal abortion, and programs to benefit children and the elderly. She also instilled in all Canadian women a closer connection to their government. Five months after becoming prime minister, Campbell and the Progressive Conservative Party suffered a terrible defeat at the polls. The party held on to just two seats in the House of Commons, and Campbell was out. But of the 295 seats in parliament, 53 were won by women, their best showing ever in Canadian politics. Kim Campbell, even in defeat and disappointment, had helped secure a victory for women.

Benazir Bhutto

First Woman Prime
Minister of Pakistan
1953–

*B*enazir Bhutto is the first woman ever elected prime minister of a Muslim nation. It is a remarkable accomplishment, for Muslim women have few rights in areas dominated by religious fundamentalists, and, in some places, their very lives are considered disposable. But it took more than a strong will for Bhutto to seek the office. It took unthinkable courage. That office was once occupied by her father, Zulfikar Ali Bhutto, before he was taken from his home, jailed, and hanged.

Benazir Bhutto was born on June 21, 1953, in Karachi, located in what was then called West Pakistan. She was the oldest of four children. Her mother was Zulfikar's second wife, Nusrat. Both parents emphasized education, and Benazir was sent, at age five, to the Convent of Jesus and Mary. As she grew, Benazir learned about the Muslim religion, even as she learned to speak English. But her father released her from many of the practices to which many Muslim women were bound. For example, the Koran (the Muslim book of holy scriptures) requires that a woman wear a veil, called *burqa,* when in public. Its purpose is to prevent supposed unwanted sexual attraction. When Nusrat first draped her oldest daughter in the traditional black gauze, Zulfikar decided Benazir didn't need to wear it. "The Prophet himself said that the best veil is the veil behind the eyes," he declared quietly. "Let her be judged by her character and her mind, not by her clothing."

In 1969, Benazir attended Harvard University, where for the first time in her life she was with people who did not know about her family, or even her country. That was to change within a year. In December 1970, Benazir's father and his Pakistan People's Party swept the elections in West Pakistan. However, the victory, which the Bhuttos hoped would help unite a divided Pakistan, brought the nation to the brink of civil war. In East Pakistan, Sheik Mujib ur-Rahman called for rebellion against the government and a complete separation from the western federation. When the military was summoned to quell the insurrection, war, which had smoldered for so long, ignited. West Pakistan struck at rebel forces in the newly named Bangladesh. Then, with millions of Bangladeshis fleeing across its borders, India attacked the two fighting nations sitting on its shoulders. By December 3, 1971, India and Pakistan were at war. Reading about the bloodshed and destruction in American newspapers, Benazir could only sit in her college dorm and worry about her family and her country. On December 16, Pakistani troops surrendered in the east, followed by a cease-fire in the west the next day. By the time the fighting had stopped, a million people had died. Pakistan had lost 5,000 square miles of territory. Ninety-three thousand Pakistani men were being held as prisoners of war in India. And the treasury had been depleted. Such were the circumstances when Zulfikar Ali Bhutto became president of Pakistan on December 20, 1971.

When a new constitution was adopted, Zulfikar Ali Bhutto became prime minister in 1973. He was overthrown by a military coup in July 1977. He was accused of ordering the murder of one of his political rivals and was thrown into jail. Nusrat assumed the leadership of the Pakistan People's Party.

Meanwhile, Benazir had graduated cum laude from Harvard in 1973 with a degree in government. She went on to Oxford, where she was elected president of the university's famous debating society, an office once held by her father. In 1977, Benazir headed back to Pakistan, expecting to join its political leadership and help institute beneficial reforms. Instead she was arrested and jailed numerous times over the next several years. Her father was executed in 1979. Benazir was subjected to solitary confinement and physical abuse, including surgery, supposedly for uterine cancer, which she later came to believe was unnecessary. In January 1984, she went to London for treatment of a severe ear infection. She was allowed to return to Pakistan in 1986 when General Mohammed Zia ul-Haq, the military ruler, lifted his ban on political opposition. Support for Bhutto had grown during her years of exile, and enthusiastic crowds welcomed her back.

In 1987, Bhutto married Asif Zardari, a Pakistani businessman. The marriage had been arranged, and Benazir saw it as a smart political move. But it also eventually grew into a strong relationship and produced three children.

General Zia was killed in a plane crash in 1988. In December, Bhutto was elected prime minister. Her mother had been elected to parliament during the autumn elections. But the new prime minister was restricted by her own promises. She had pledged not to reduce the military budget, which drained money away from much-needed social programs. Bhutto won more freedom for the press, as well as trade unions and student groups. But without a majority in either house of parliament, she had little political strength. On August 6, 1990, Pakistan's president threw Bhutto out of office.

Bhutto held her seat as opposition leader in the parliament. And three years later, she was named prime minister again after elections in October 1993. However, violence once again followed Benazir as her brother, Murtaza, also a member of parliament, was killed in 1996, after being arrested by police. In November 1996, Benazir was removed from office by the president, and her husband was arrested for political and financial corruption. She continues the fight to clear her name.

Activists

We don't know if women conducted organized protests for their rights in ancient times. It would probably be safe to say that they didn't. They were restricted by modes of communication and transportation, not to mention the fear of being beheaded or drowned in mud. Through the Middle Ages and the Renaissance, women were trapped in lives of monotony, limitation, and persecution.

In the late eighteenth century, the manufacture of many products was moved out of the home and into factories. There, goods could be turned out quickly and uniformly by amazing new machines designed for mass production. A very large percentage of the workers in those factories were female. As part of a large group, probably for the first time in their lives, workers began to share ideas and feelings. They expressed their desire for shorter hours, higher pay, and better working conditions. Workers began to unite, replacing the powerlessness of the individual with the power of the group. But women soon recognized that even within their circle of peers, men and women were treated differently. Men often received higher pay for the same work performed by the women. Hiring and firing practices were not equal. Gradually, women banded together, formed organizations, spoke out, went on strike, protested, held rallies. The woman's suffrage movement was born.

Irish independence activist Bernadette Devlin McAliskey speaks to wives of Irish prisoners outside the Houses of Parliament in this 1971 photo. McAliskey was the youngest person ever elected to the British Parliament.

But even the ability to vote and hold elected office did not bring equal rights to women. In virtually every nation, women make up more than half the population. Yet no country on earth has ever had a government in which women were represented in proportions that even approached 50 percent. Just as there is strength in numbers in the factory, there is also strength in numbers in parliament, courts, and political parties. When men dominate the government, women's issues can easily be ignored. In the United States, that means continued mistreatment in the workplace, the armed services, and even in the home. In other nations, it may mean violence, poverty, and starvation as a way of life.

Wherever there is injustice, there will always be brave people who will stand up in protest. Facing jail, torture, and death, these men and women express the outrage felt by the many others who are unable or unwilling to speak out. They protest discrimination, corruption, and war. They have no weapons and no political power. Yet, using little more than their minds and voices, they make a difference.

There have been thousands of such reformers throughout history in countries around the world. Many were silenced, and remain anonymous. Here are three we know about.

Gloria Steinem

Author, Publisher, Activist
1934–

"I once thought I would do this for two or three years and then go home to my real life," Gloria Steinem once said. But she had underestimated the complexity of the situation. She believed that if women simply pointed out their problems, everyone, even men, would surely want to help fix them. Now, after more than a quarter century at the front lines, Gloria Steinem is still the most powerful symbol for the battle women continue to fight. But she is much more: she is a symbol of the positive change that is possible for all members of society who face injustice.

Gloria Steinem was born on March 25, 1934, in Toledo, Ohio. Her father was Leo Steinem, a childlike man who was a fountain of inventions, ad slogans, and product ideas. One of them, he was always sure, would someday make him rich. He died in 1962, still believing that. (Leo's mother, Pauline, had served as president of the Ohio Women's Suffrage Association from 1908 to 1911.) Gloria's mother, Ruth Nunevillar Steinem, was a teacher and journalist. At age thirty, she gave up her career to help her husband run the summer resort they owned in Michigan. She suffered through several nervous breakdowns and died in 1980.

Many of Gloria's early years were spent in a house trailer, traveling the country as Leo searched for his fortune. When Gloria was twelve, her parents divorced. She returned to Toledo with her mother, where they lived in a rat-infested basement apartment. Still battling the effects of her first breakdown, Ruth was unable to care even for herself. In many ways, Gloria assumed the role of parent in what was to be the most difficult period of her life. During her senior year, Gloria went to live with her sister in Washington, D.C., while Leo stayed in Toledo to care for Ruth. In 1952, Gloria enrolled in Smith College, where she majored in government, was elected to Phi Beta Kappa, and graduated magna cum laude. After graduation, she went to India to study at the University of Delhi. She began to publish newspaper articles and wrote a guidebook for the Indian government.

Steinem returned to the United States in 1958. Two years later, she landed a job writing photo captions for a political magazine. Then, in 1963, she went undercover to work as a waitress in a Playboy club in New York City. The article that resulted, "I Was a Playboy Bunny," attracted attention, and Steinem's journalism career took off. She published articles on various social causes in *Cosmopolitan*, *McCall's*, *Glamour*, and *Vogue*. She also wrote for television. In the process, she became something of a celebrity. Then, in 1968, she was asked to write a regular column, called "The City Politic," for *New York* magazine. This assignment gave Steinem access to the inner workings of local and national government, as well as the grassroots movements of the time. She became involved in Cesar Chavez's efforts on behalf of California farm workers. She began actively protesting the war in Vietnam. And she supported the presidential campaigns of Eugene McCarthy and Robert F. Kennedy.

In February 1969, Steinem attended a meeting held by a women's group called the Redstockings. The topic of discussion was illegal abortion, a subject Steinem knew something about: she had had an abortion shortly after college. She discovered that her feelings of guilt, shame, and oppression were shared by many women—and that those feelings were being generated, or at least magnified, by the attitudes and policies of government and society. She also realized that her mother had surrendered her own dreams in order to fit the role society expected of her, which resulted in a complete emotional breakdown. Steinem began to write articles, give lectures, and appear on television and radio talk shows. In 1971, she joined Bella Abzug, Shirley Chisholm, and Betty Friedan to found the National Women's Political Caucus, an organization dedicated to getting more women to run for office.

Then Steinem met Dorothy Pitman Hughes, an African-American who had founded one of the first community day-care centers in New York City. Both women saw the need to bridge the gap between white and nonwhite women, and they established the Women's Action Alliance. Together, they spoke out in support of legalized abortion, equal pay for equal work, and the Equal Rights Amendment. Steinem also began making plans to publish a magazine concerned with the emerging feminist consciousness. The magazine would be owned and edited by women.

The first issue of *Ms.* magazine was a thirty-page insert in the December 1971 issue of *New York*. The following month, *Ms.* was a separate publication and sold out its three hundred thousand copies in a week. By the mid-1970s, the magazine had a readership of half a million and featured articles such as, "Down with Sexist Upbringing" and "Why Women Fear Success." The magazine has been bought and sold several times since then and is now published without advertisements, supported solely by its two hundred thousand readers.

Steinem continues to write for *Ms.,* as well as other publications. She is also a popular speaker and is active in several causes related to women's issues. Her many books include *Wonder Woman* (1972), *Outrageous Acts and Everyday Rebellions* (1983), *Marilyn: Norma Jean* (1986), *Revolution from Within* (1992), and *Moving Beyond Words* (1994). In 1993, Steinem was inducted into the National Women's Hall of Fame in Seneca Falls.

Aung San Suu Kyi

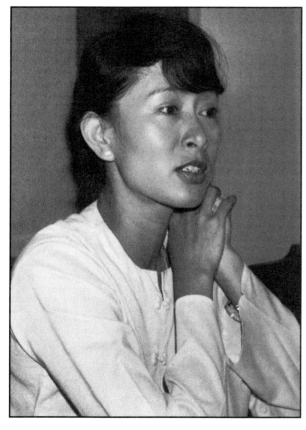

Civil Rights Leader,
Myanmar
1945–

*W*hat does it take to bring down a powerful military regime? Obviously, a force more powerful. That could mean concentrated military strength or scattered revolutionary violence. Or it could mean people united in pride for their nation, citizens with the courage to resist and a willingness to suffer. Sometimes it means communication and knowledge. Almost always, it means a passion for liberty that can only be sparked by a leader with vision and devotion, someone who knows when action is necessary, and when patience is best.

Aung San Suu Kyi was born on June 19, 1945, in Rangoon, the capital of what is now Myanmar (formerly Burma). She was the youngest of three children born to Aung San and Daw Khin Kyi. Her father, Aung San, led the movement toward Burmese independence after three years of Japanese rule and more than a century of intervention and domination by the British. On January 4, 1948, the Union of Burma was created. Aung San had won a place in his country's history books. But his own daughter would never know him: he was assassinated, along with eight members of his executive council, in 1947.

After a constitutional democracy was set up in 1948, the government immediately went about trying to protect itself from revolutionaries. One tactic was to build a large military, which drove away the rebels but also began abusing the power it had acquired. In 1958, the ruling Anti-Fascist People's Freedom League (which had been founded by Aung San) was torn apart by disagreement. Prime Minister Nu asked General Ne Win to help him hold new elections. In 1960, those elections returned Nu to power. But two years later, Ne Win overthrew the government and ruled Burma for the next twenty-six years. His dictatorship gave way to a constitutional government, but it amounted to nothing more than another military dictatorship dressed up to look like a democracy. Ne Win and the military controlled all aspects of Burmese life, including education and communication. Anyone suspected of antigovernment feelings was arrested. Visitors were all but kept out of the country. Unemployment soared.

As the economy continued to decline, violence erupted. Burma was in a constant state of civil war. In July 1988, Ne Win resigned as head of his party. He was replaced by another military leader. Since then, the nation has endured an uninterrupted series of repressive leaders, violent protests, and new governments.

By the time Ne Win had assumed control of the government in 1960, Aung San Suu Kyi had moved to New Delhi, where her mother was Burma's ambassador to India. While in India, Suu Kyi took riding lessons and learned to play the piano. She also studied the teachings of Mohandas Gandhi, who had promoted a life of nonviolent civil disobedience in British-ruled India. In 1964, Suu Kyi entered Oxford University, where she studied politics, philosophy, and economics. She received her bachelor's degree in 1967. At Oxford, she met Michael Aris, and they were married in 1972. After some time in the Himalayan kingdom of Bhutan, the couple returned to England. In 1973, Suu Ky gave birth to a son, named Alexander. Four years later, their second son, Kim, was born.

While living in England, Suu Kyi developed a strong interest in her father. She began researching the details of his life and writing about them in essays, and eventually in a book called *Freedom from Fear*. Suu Kyi had always known she might someday return to Burma to serve her homeland. In April 1988, she arrived in Rangoon to take care of her dying mother. The capital city was tense. Riot police and students were clashing frequently, and many students had been killed. In August, massive demonstrations against a political appointment brought out the army, which fired randomly into the crowded streets, killing thousands. Inspired by her father's memory, Aung San Suu Kyi addressed a crowd of a half million people at a sacred shrine in Rangoon. Her resemblance to her father and the words she used to describe "Burma's second struggle for independence" inspired the people to follow her leadership. Although she repeatedly reminded the crowds of the essential role of the military, its leaders saw Suu Kyi as a threat. Perhaps to make room in the prisons for those arrested for political activities, the government released five thousand inmates, who then proceeded to loot stores and homes.

The military responded by reasserting its control over the government. It banned all political gatherings. It also announced that it would arrest and sentence people without the benefit of trial. When thousands of people took to the streets in protest, soldiers shot at the crowd. Meanwhile, Suu Kyi was traveling from village to village, urging the people of Burma to continue the fight for freedom and human rights. By October, she was speaking to crowds of tens of thousands, and by the following June, she was openly referring to the government leaders as fascists who must be resisted. On July 20, 1989, Suu Kyi was placed under house arrest. She was not permitted to leave her home and was allowed only occasional visits by her husband and sons. In 1991, she was awarded the Nobel Peace Prize. She was released from house arrest on July 10, 1995. She continues to speak to crowds at her home, just as the government continues to harass and arrest her followers. Although the military dictatorship is still in power, Aung San Suu Kyi keeps the flame of democracy alive in Myanmar.

Bernadette Devlin McAliskey

Northern Ireland's Civil Rights Leader
1947–

Bernadette Devlin Mc-Aliskey knew that the struggle between the Protestants and Catholics in Northern Ireland would not be settled quickly, or peacefully. The fighting had been going on for years, centuries in fact, and would surely continue until some drastic changes were made. When she became a member of the British Parliament at age twenty-one, perhaps she thought, briefly, that change was at hand. Now, nearly a legend in her homeland, McAliskey continues to fight for change and to hope for peace.

Bernadette Josephine Devlin was born on April 23, 1947, in Dungannon,

County Tyrone, Northern Ireland. The third of six children, she discovered early in life what it was like to live as a second-class citizen. Her father, John James Devlin, was the son of a road sweeper. Her mother, Elizabeth Bernadette, came from a prominent and somewhat powerful family that did not approve of her marriage. As a result, the Devlins had few friends and were forced to live as outcasts in their own town. Bernadette suffered from poor health as a baby, struggling with bronchial and lumbar pneumonia, as well as asthma.

John James was a carpenter and a political agitator who read his children anti-British bedtime stories from books on Irish history and folklore. Northern Ireland had been divided from the rest of the country since 1920, when Britain passed the Government of Ireland Act and set up a separate parliament in Ireland's six northern counties. Southern Ireland became known as the Free State, where Roman Catholics represented a large majority of the population. Not wishing to be dominated by the Catholics in the south, Northern Ireland's mostly Protestant population chose to remain part of Great Britain. In the north, Roman Catholics comprised only about one-third of the population. They had long been discriminated against in many areas of society. For example, voting laws requiring property ownership kept Catholics from choosing leaders who represented them. When a business had to lay off employees, the Catholics were the first to go. The Catholics blamed this situation on their minority status. They frequently protested, sometimes violently. John James Devlin, a Catholic activist, could not get work after authorities labeled him a political suspect. He was forced to live away from his family, visiting only on weekends and holidays. When he died in 1956, the Devlins had to get by on a widow's pension and a modest allowance from the state.

In October 1965, Bernadette received a government scholarship to Queen's University in Belfast, the capital of Northern Ireland. She majored in psychology and decided to become a research psychologist. In January 1967, her mother died, but Bernadette was able to remain in school when neighbors offered to help with the younger children in the family.

Then, in August 1968, Bernadette participated in a civil rights march from the town of Coalisland to Dungannon. Two months later, she watched as a young man who had tried to protect her was severely beaten by a policeman. "I was in such a state of anger that I just went back and poured forth at the students for two hours," she later said. "And I haven't stopped since." Bernadette helped organize People's Democracy, a student civil rights movement. Among its demands were an electoral system that gave each citizen exactly one vote, a system of defining electoral boundaries that did not give advantages to any one group, the right to free speech and assembly, a limitation of the police's powers of arrest, and a fair distribution of housing and jobs. Bernadette organized sit-ins and protest marches. She openly confronted militant Protestants. And she helped plan the "long march," a protest procession that spanned much of Northern Ireland, from Belfast to Londonderry, in January 1969.

In the late 1960s, Northern Ireland had twelve seats in the British Parliament. A seat in the House of Commons had become vacant after the death of George Forrest. With the election scheduled for April 17, the Republican Party offered to support Devlin. She reluctantly agreed to run, even though she had no real desire to become a member of Parliament. Her opponent was Anna Forrest, the widow of the deceased Unionist Party member. With two weeks to campaign, Bernadette visited and spoke in every town. She ran a nonreligious campaign and in the end came away with 33,648 votes to Mrs. Forrest's 29,437. On April 22, 1969, twenty-one-year-old Bernadette Devlin took her seat in the House of Commons. She was the youngest woman in history to sit as a member of Parliament.

On her very first day, Bernadette addressed the House of Commons. She criticized the Unionists for working only to preserve their own privileges, and the government for not making good on its promises of reform. Civil rights demonstrations, led in part by Devlin, continued against the government of Northern Ireland. In July, a crowd of Protestants and police invaded the Bogside, a Catholic working-class section of Londonderry. When the Irish Republican Army (IRA) joined forces with the civil rights activists to protect the area, intense fighting broke out. The British government sent troops to Londonderry and Belfast. Ever since, Northern Ireland has alternated between bloodshed and ceasefire. Thousands have died. Meanwhile, Devlin was charged with disorderly conduct and inciting a riot. Her imprisonment in June 1970 caused even more rioting. She was released four months later. She gave birth to a child in 1971 and was married in 1973. The following year she lost her bid for reelection. She has continued to work for peace in all of Ireland.

Women in
World Politics:

Miles of Progress, Miles to Go

NORTH AMERICA

In Canada, women were given the right to vote in stages, beginning in 1917. Jeanne Sauvé was named governor general in 1984. Kim Campbell became Canada's first woman prime minister in 1993. Campbell's term in office lasted just a few months, but her rise to power inspired Canadian women to become more involved in politics. In 1994, women occupied 15 percent of the seats in the upper chamber of the legislature and 18 percent in the lower chamber.

Mexico is another story. Mexican women gained the right to vote in 1947, and six years later the right to run for office. In 1982, Rosario Ibarra de Piedra became the first woman to run for president of Mexico. By 1994, 5 percent of the seats in Mexico's Senate were held by women. In the Chamber of Deputies, or lower house, women made up 8 percent of the legislators.

CENTRAL AMERICA

The most prominent story from Central America is the presidency of Violeta Chamorro of Nicaragua, which lasted for seven years. In 1994, her nation's parliament was 16 percent women—relatively high for the region. Women composed 5 percent of the legislature in Guatemala and 8 percent in Honduras and Panama. In Belize, women held 22 percent of the seats, the greatest percentage in Central America.

As with all regions, the numbers fail to tell the whole story. In many areas, minorities suffer under oppressive conditions, with little or no representation in government.

SOUTH AMERICA AND THE CARIBBEAN

The continent of South America consists of twelve independent nations and one territory (French Guiana is governed by France). Each of the twelve nations has a president. In addition, Peru and Guyana have prime ministers. Two women have been elected president: Isabel Perón of Argentina in 1974, and Lidia Gueiler Tejada of Bolivia in 1979. Perón was the world's first female president, and the first to be thrown out of office in a military coup; she held office for two years. Tejada served for one year and was also ousted in a coup.

In the legislatures, Guyana has the highest percentage of women, with 20 percent. Argentina is next with about 16 percent. Ecuador's parliament contains 5 percent women. Uruguay has no women in the upper chamber and 6 percent in the lower, matching the legislature of Suriname.

The Caribbean Sea is home to hundreds of islands, some of them independent nations. Eugenia Charles was elected prime minister of Dominica in 1980 and remained in office for fifteen years. In 1991, Ertha Pascal-Trouillot was elected president of Haiti.

In 1994, St. Lucia women constituted 36 percent of the legislature's upper house. In Barbados, they held 29 percent of the seats in the upper chamber. The women in Trinidad and Tobago had reached about 23 percent in the upper house and 14 percent in the lower. At the lower extreme, Haiti had no women in the upper chamber and 4 percent in the lower.

ASIA

Asia is a vast continent of nations with long histories. Until the late twentieth century, change came slowly to these lands. Catherine the Great was empress of Russia for more than thirty-four years. Tz'u-hsi was empress of China for forty-seven. For hundreds of years, countries such as Tibet, India, Mongolia, and Vietnam remained isolated, and were sources of mystery to the West.

But in the twentieth century, change came quickly almost everywhere. Japan, Taiwan, Hong Kong, Singapore, and Korea became manufacturing giants in a few short decades. Communism appeared, completely overwhelmed the lives of millions of Asians and Europeans, then disappeared seemingly overnight. The state of Israel was born, and almost immediately fighting broke out between the new nation and its neighbors; it has rarely stopped for long. In politics, governments changed hands through violent acts by the military, religious fanatics, or revolutionaries. Prime Minister Indira Gandhi of India was assassinated in 1984; seven years later, her son Rajiv, the former prime minister, was also murdered. In the Philippines, Benigno Aquino was gunned down by the government with such predictability that it was almost like watching an old movie.

Through it all, women have struggled against violence, kidnapping, imprisonment, and social discrimination. Yet, they have also made unexpected political gains. Corazon Aquino picked up where her husband left off and became president of the Philippines. Tansu Çiller was elected prime minister of Turkey. Benazir Bhutto was elected prime minister of Pakistan. Sirimavo Bandaranaike became prime minister of Sri Lanka in 1960 and again in 1994.

In Myanmar, Aung San Suu Kyi resisted the continual cycle of military dictatorships tormenting that nation's people. And in Indonesia, riots broke out when opposition party leader Megawati Sukarniputri was removed by force.

The populations of many Asian nations are growing quickly, like an inflating balloon. Everywhere in Asia, as in the rest of the world, women's participation in government is somehow stifled. No Asian nation has more than 21 percent of the seats in its legislature occupied by women. And most have far fewer. In Pakistan, Lebanon, Azerbaijan, and Turkey, women represent 2 percent of the lawmakers. In South Korea, female representation is 1 percent. In Kuwait, women can neither vote nor run for office.

AFRICA

Africa consists of more than fifty countries. Tiny nations fit, like pieces of stained glass, in the spaces between enormous nations. (Algeria is one-fourth the size of Europe. Rwanda is smaller than Massachusetts.) Advances in technology and industry have not overcome widespread poverty and disease. In government, model democracies exist side-by-side with dangerous military dictatorships. Assassinations and unexplained deaths are common among national leaders.

For African women in politics, progress has been slow and difficult. They have been caught among the conflicts between black and white, rich and poor, urban and rural, this group and that. In the process, they have gained little political power. Between 1987 and 1994, the number of women holding seats in national legislatures increased by 1 percent.

The first notable female head of state in Africa lived more than two millenia ago. Her name was Cleopatra and she ruled Egypt. But she was actually Greek, and most of her influence took place in Europe and Asia.

In modern Africa, two woman have served as prime ministers, and each governed for just a few months. Sylvie Kinigi of Burundi served as prime minister from October 1993 until February 1994. Her term fell in the middle of much political turmoil that included the assassination of the nation's president. After her cabinet fell apart, Kinigi resigned and went to work for a bank.

In Rwanda, Agathe Uwilingiyimana was a leader of her nation's women's movement. She fought to end the oppression of women and their exclusion from politics. After five months as prime minister, Uwilingiyimana was assassinated on April 6, 1994, by members of the presidential guard.

The year Uwilingiyimana was killed, 17 percent of the seats in Rwanda's national legislature were held by women. Neighboring Uganda also had 17 percent. Only the extremely small island nation of Seychelles, with 27 percent, and South Africa, with 25 percent, were higher. In more than thirty African countries, female representation in the legislature was less than 10 percent. In Ethiopia, where fifty-seven million people struggle to live, women made up 1 percent of the lawmaking body. Mauritania's two-chamber legislature had no women.

AUSTRALIA AND NEW ZEALAND

Women constitute about 21 percent of Australia's upper house of parliament. In the lower house, women occupy about 8 percent of the seats. (Aboriginal women, restricted by complex voting requirements, have virtually no representation.) In New Zealand, women hold about 21 percent of the seats in the legislature. The other island nations in the region show even less representation by women. In Indonesia, it's 12 percent, and in Papua New Guinea, zero.

What explanations are there for such low numbers after all these years? The likely one is that many men in the region still believe women do not belong in government. Given that more than half the population is female, it appears that many women feel the same way. Unfortunately, without enough advocates in parliament, the issues affecting women in Australia, New Zealand, and the surrounding islands will continue to receive inadequate attention.

EUROPE

In 1994, the Scandinavian nations continued to lead the way in female representation in legislatures. Finland's parliament is 39 percent women, as is Norway's. Sweden and Denmark follow close behind with 34 and 33 percent, respectively.

At the other end of the spectrum is the tiny island-nation of Malta, south of Sicily, which has a female representation in parliament of about 2 percent. Romania, Belarus, and the Ukraine have about 4 percent, and Bosnia-Herzegovina has 5. Only slightly higher, with 6 percent, are Albania, Croatia, France, Greece, and Monaco.

Europe has a long history of female monarchs. Some queens were objects of worship among their people. Others were nothing short of tyrants. More recently, European nations have elected five woman prime ministers: Margaret Thatcher of Great Britain, Gro Harlem Brundtland of Norway, Maria de Lourdes Pintasilgo of Portugal, Edith Cresson of France, and Hanna Suchocka of Poland. Two women have served as presidents: Vigdis Finnbogadottir of Iceland and Agatha Barbara of Malta.

Important Dates in Women's Political History

51 B.C.	Cleopatra VII ascends the throne of Egypt.
1474	Isabella I is crowned queen of Castile, Spain.
1542	Mary, Queen of Scots, ascends the throne of Scotland when she is six days old.
1559	Catherine de Médicis is named regent of France.
1762	Catherine the Great begins a thirty-four-year reign as empress of Russia.
1837	Victoria I ascends the throne to begin a sixty-four-year reign as queen of England.
1862	Sojourner Truth helps former slaves find jobs and housing in Virginia.
1869	The territory of Wyoming gives women the vote.
	Elizabeth Cady Stanton becomes the first president of the National Woman Suffrage Association.
1872	Susan B. Anthony is arrested after casting a vote in Rochester, New York.

1891   Liliuokalani becomes the last queen of Hawaii.

1893   Women in New Zealand win the right to vote.

1900   Under Empress Tz'u-hsi, foreigners and missionaries are driven out of China.

1906   Women in Finland are the first in Europe to vote.

1916   Jeannette Rankin from Montana is the first woman elected to the U.S. Congress.

1920   The Nineteenth Amendment gives women in the United States the right to vote.

        League of Women Voters is founded.

1923   Aleksandra Kollontai of Russia becomes the first woman accredited as an ambassador.

1945   Eleanor Roosevelt is appointed to the United States delegation to the UN.

1948   Margaret Chase Smith becomes the first American woman elected to both the House and Senate.

1951   Eva Perón runs for vice president of Argentina.

1960   Sirimavo Bandaranaike of Sri Lanka becomes the world's first woman prime minister.

        Nakayama Masa becomes Japan's first woman cabinet minister.

1967   Indira Gandhi is elected prime minister of India.

1968   Shirley Chisholm becomes the first African-American woman elected to the United States Congress.

1969   Golda Meir, age seventy-one, becomes prime minister of Israel.

        Bernadette Devlin, age twenty-one, takes a seat in Britain's House of Commons.

1970   Bella Abzug is elected to the first of three terms in Congress from New York City.

1971   Gloria Steinem founds *Ms.* magazine; joins Abzug, Chisholm, and Betty Friedan in founding the National Women's Political Caucus.

1974   Isabel Martinez de Perón is elected first woman president of Argentina.

        Ella Grasso is elected governor of Connecticut.

1976   Congresswoman Barbara Jordan delivers the keynote speech at the Democratic National Convention.

1978   Nancy Kassebaum of Kansas is the first woman elected to the U.S. Senate without following in her husband's footsteps.

1979   Margaret Thatcher becomes Great Britain's first woman prime minister.

        Jane Byrne becomes the first woman mayor of Chicago.

        Dianne Feinstein is first woman elected mayor of San Francisco.

        Maria de Lourdes Pintasilgo becomes Portugal's first woman prime minister.

        Lidia Gueiler Tejada becomes first woman president of Bolivia.

1980   Eugenia Charles becomes the first woman prime minister of Dominica.

        Vigdis Finnbogadottir of Iceland becomes Europe's first female president.

        Jeane Kirkpatrick becomes the first female United States ambassador to the UN.

1981   Sandra Day O'Connor becomes the first woman on the U.S. Supreme Court.

        Gro Harlem Brundtland becomes Norway's first female prime minister.

1982   Agatha Barbara becomes the first woman president of Malta.

1984   Geraldine Ferraro becomes the first woman to run for vice president of the United States on a major party ticket.

        Madeleine Kunin is elected governor of Vermont.

1985   Wilma Mankiller becomes the first woman chief of the Cherokee Nation.

1986   Corazon Aquino becomes first woman elected president of the Philippines.

        Barbara Mikulski is elected senator from Maryland.

1989   Aung San Suu Kyi is placed under house arrest in Myanmar.

1990   Violeta Chamorro is elected as Nicaragua's first woman president.

        Ann Richards is elected governor of Texas.

        Mary Robinson becomes the first woman president of Ireland.

1991   Edith Cresson becomes France's first woman prime minister.

        Khaleda Zia Rahman becomes the first female prime minister of Bangladesh.

1992   Dianne Feinstein and Barbara Boxer become the first women serving in the U.S. Senate from the same state at the same time.

        Carol Moseley-Braun is the first African-American woman elected to the U.S. Senate.

        Hanna Suchocka becomes Poland's first woman prime minister.

1993   Kim Campbell is elected Canada's first woman prime minister.

        Agathe Uwilingiyimana becomes Rwanda's first woman prime minister.

Sylvie Kinigi becomes Burundi's first woman prime minister.

Benazir Bhutto is elected prime minister of Pakistan for the second time.

Tansu Çiller becomes prime minister of Turkey.

Hillary Clinton is named chair of the Task Force on National Health Care Reform.

Christie Whitman is elected governor of New Jersey.

1994   Chandrika Bandaranaike Kumaratunga becomes president of Sri Lanka. She appoints her mother, Sirimavo Bandaranaike, prime minister.

Pat Schroeder of Colorado is elected to her twelfth consecutive term in the U.S. House of Representatives.

After eight terms in the House, Olympia Snowe is elected a senator from Maine.

1996   Madeleine Albright is the first woman to become U.S. secretary of state.

Ruth Perry becomes Liberia's chair of the council of state.

Organizations and Online Sites

Australian Democrats
10-12 Brisbane Avenue
Barton ACT 2600
http://www.democrats.org.au/
Group dedicated to serving the best interests of all Australians—and all world citizens.

Barbara Boxer
http://www.senate.gov/~boxer/
Biography of the California senator, news, services, and links to pages on various issues.

Barbara Mikulski
http://www.senate.gov/~mikulski/
Learn about the Maryland senator's life, career, committee assignments, and voting record.

Black Women's Agenda
3501 14th Street, NW
Washington, DC 20010
202-387-4166

Carol Moseley-Braun
http://www.senate.gov/~moseley-braun/
The Illinois senator's home page, featuring a biography, her legislative record, and links to resources.

Center for Advancement of Public Policy
1735 S Street, NW
Washington, DC 20009
202-797-0606

Center for the American Woman in Politics
Eagleton Institute of Politics
Rutgers University
New Brunswick, NJ 08901
908-828-2210

Dianne Feinstein
http://www.senate.gov/~feinstein/
Learn all about the former San Francisco mayor and current California senator, as well as news about issues and legislation.

Eleanor Roosevelt National Historic Site
519 Albany Post Road
Hyde Park, NY 12538
http://www.nps.gov/elro/home-txt.html
Lots of information about the buildings and grounds, events, biography, and related links.

The Feminist Majority
1600 Wilson Blvd., Suite 801
Arlington, VA 22209
http://www.feminist.org/home.html
News, current events, and information about a wide variety of issues of concern to women, including health, education, politics, arts, entertainment, and sports.

50/50 By 2000
Box 34
Fairfield, CT 06430
203-259-1446

Hillary Rodham Clinton
http://www.whitehouse.gov/WH/EOP/First_Lady/html/HILLARY_Home.html
Meet the First Lady, read her columns and speeches, find out about the programs that she's involved in, flip through a photo scrapbook, learn about life in the White House, and plenty more.

Hispanas Organized for Political Equality (HOPE)
3220 East 26th Street
Vernon, CA 90023
213-267-5853

House of Representatives
http://www.house.gov/
News, member information, votes, recap of the past week's activities, committees, schedules, and the legislative process.

Justices of the Supreme Court
http://www.usscplus.com/info/index.htm
Photos and biographies of each of the nine justices, plus links to information about the Court, its history, and procedures.

League of Women Voters
1730 M Street NW
Washington, DC 20036-4508
http://www.lwv.org/
National group working to increase participation of all citizens in government, and to influence public policy through various activities.

Madeleine Albright
http://secretary.state.gov/
All about the secretary of state's life and job, including her travels, current issues, quotes, and photos.

Mexican American Women's National Association
1101 17th Street, NW
Suite 803
Washington, DC 20036-4704
202-833-0060

Most Powerful Women in the World
http://wisdom.psinet.net.au/~lani/100mpw.html
Link to the biographies of the one hundred most powerful women on the planet (according to *Australian Magazine*). Learn about everyone from Sandra Day O'Connor to Madonna, and find out where they rank.

***Ms.* Magazine**
http://www.womweb.com/index.html
Learn about current issues, activities, people, and links to other sites.

National Council of Jewish Women
53 West 23rd Street
New York, NY 10010
http://www.ncjw.org/
Strives to improve services and conditions for women, children, and families through local, state, and national activities.

National Council of Negro Women
1001 G Street NW, Suite 800
Washington, DC 20001
http://www.ncnw.org/
Programs aimed at improving the quality of life for African-American women and their families. Learn about the group's worldwide activities, as well as a wide variety of resources.

National Organization for Women (NOW)
1000 16th Street, NW, Suite 700
Washington, DC 20036
http://www.now.org/
An online meeting place for women dealing with a vast array of social and political issues. Features plenty of information, resources, and related links.

National Woman's Party
144 Constitution Avenue, NE
Washington, DC 20002
202-546-1210

National Women's Hall of Fame
76 Fall Street
Seneca Falls, NY 13148
http://www.greatwomen.org/
Visit the nation's first organization to celebrate the achievements of women. You'll find a history of women in the United States, a calendar of events, gift shop, and information on new inductees, as well as existing members.

National Women's Law Center
1616 P Street, NW
Suite 100
Washington, DC 20036
202-328-5160

National Women's Political Caucus
1211 Connecticut Avenue, Suite 425
Washington, DC 20036
http://www.feminist.com/nwpc.htm
Dedicated to increasing the number of women elected and appointed to political office. This site includes links to publications, current events, "Good Guy Awards," and more.

Older Women's League (OWL)
666 11th Street, NW
Suite 700
Washington, DC 20001
202-783-6686
800-825-3695

Olympia Snowe
http://www.senate.gov/~snowe/
Biography, committee assignments, helpful tips for visitors to Washington, DC, email, an oral message from the senator, and lots of information about Maine.

Organization of Pan-Asian American Women
P.O. Box 39128
Washington, DC 20016
202-659-9370

Patty Murray
http://www.senate.gov/~murray/
Biography, current legislation, information on Washington State, and a special section, "Just for Young People."

20%+ By 2020
255 West Julian Street
Suite 100
San Jose, CA 93110-2406
408-287-1700

The White House
http://www.whitehouse.gov/WH/Welcome.html
News, photos, and tons of information about the White House and its occupants, past and present.

Women in Politics

http://www.lib.lsu.edu/soc/women.html

Features biographies on current and past women world leaders, a quiz, and lots of links to related organizations.

Women Leaders Online

http://wlo.org/

"The first and largest women's advocacy group created on the Internet." News, discussion groups, links, and more.

Women's Action Coalition (WAC)

P.O. Box 1862
Chelsea Station
New York, NY 10113-0950
212-967-7711, ext. WACM

Women's Action for New Directions (WAND)

305 7th Street, SE
Washington, DC 20003
202-543-8505

Women's Campaign Fund

120 Maryland Avenue, NE
Washington, DC 20002
202-544-4484
http://www.wowfactor.com/WCF/
Learn about this group's activities as it strives to support women candidates.

Women's International League for Peace and Freedom

1213 Race Street
Philadelphia, PA 19107
215-563-7110

For Further Reading

Altman, Susan, *Extraordinary Black Americans* (Danbury, Conn.: Children's Press, 1989).

Ashby, Ruth, and Deborah Gore Ohrn, eds., *Herstory* (New York: Viking, 1995).

Harrison, Pat, *Jeane Kirkpatrick* (New York: Chelsea House, 1991).

Bhutto, Benazir, *Daughter of Destiny* (New York: Simon & Schuster, 1989).

Braden, Maria, *Women Politicians and the Media* (Lexington: University Press of Kentucky, 1987).

Bradford, Ernle, *Cleopatra* (San Diego, Calif.: Harcourt Brace Jovanovich, 1972).

Brill, Alida, ed., *A Rising Public Voice* (New York: Feminist Press, 1995).

Bysiewicz, Susan, *Ella* (Marblehead, Mass.: Peregrine Press, 1984).

Campbell, Kim, *Time and Chance* (Toronto: McClelland-Bantam, 1996).

Erickson, Carolly, *Great Catherine* (New York: Crown, 1994).

Faber, Doris, *Bella Abzug* (New York: Lothrop, Lee & Shepard, 1976).

Fraser, Antonia, *The Warrior Queens* (New York: Alfred A. Knopf, 1989).

Gibbs, Richard, *Women Prime Ministers* (Parsippany, N.J.: Silver Burdett Company, 1982).

Hoobler, Dorothy, and Thomas Hoobler, *Cleopatra* (New York: Chelsea House, 1988).

King, Norman, *The Woman in the White House: The Remarkable Story of Hillary Rodham Clinton* (Secaucus, N.J.: Carol, 1996).

Komisar, Lucy, *Corazon Aquino: The Story of a Revolution* (New York: George Braziller, 1987).

Kunin, Madeleine, *Living a Political Life* (New York: Alfred A. Knopf, 1994).

Le Veness, Frank P., and Jane P. Sweeney, eds., *Women Leaders in Contemporary U.S. Politics* (Sterling, Va.: Reiner, 1987).

Lee, Richard, and Mary Price Lee, *Careers for Women in Politics* (New York: Rosen, 1989).

Liswood, Laura A., *Women World Leaders* (New York: HarperCollins, 1995).

Macht, Norman L., *Sandra Day O'Connor, Supreme Court Justice* (New York: Chelsea House, 1992).

McClure, Sandy, *For the People* (New York: Prometheus, 1996).

Meir, Golda, *My Life* (New York: Dell, 1975).

Mullen, Richard, and James Munson, Victoria, *Portrait of a Queen* (London: BBC Books, 1987).

Radcliffe, Donnie, *Hillary Rodham Clinton: A First Lady for Our Time* (New York: Warner Books, 1993).

Roeder, Ralph, *Catherine de Médicis and the Lost Revolution* (New York: Viking, 1937).

Roosevelt, Eleanor, *The Autobiography of Eleanor Roosevelt* (New York: G. K. Hall, 1984).

Trease, Geoffrey, *Seven Sovereign Queens* (New York: Vanguard Press, 1968).

Wallace, Patricia Ward, *Politics of Conscience: A Biography of Margaret Chase Smith* (New York: Praeger, 1995).

Whitney, Sharon, and Tom Raynor, *Women in Politics* (Danbury, Conn.: Franklin Watts, 1986).

Williams, Barbara, *Breakthrough: Women In Politics* (New York: Walker, 1979).

Wilson, Hazel, *Liliuokalani: Last Queen of Hawaii* (New York: Alfred A. Knopf, 1963).

Index

abolitionist movement, 46

Abzug, Bella, 114–117
  and Vietnam War, 116

Africa, 48, 49, 262, 263

Albert, Prince of Saxe-Coburg.
  See Victoria I

Albright, Madeleine, 196–199
  as president of Center for National
    Policy, 198
  as U.S. ambassador to United
    Nations, 198–199
  as U.S. secretary of state, 199
  *Poland: The Role of the Press in Political
    Change* (author), 198

American Equal Rights Association, 55

American Woman Suffrage
  Association, 57

ancient Egypt, 17, 18, 20.
  See also Cleopatra VII

ancient Greece, 17

Anthony, Susan Brownell, 13, 46, 53,
  54–57
  and abolitionist movement, 54, 55
  and temperance movement, 55.
    See also Stanton, Elizabeth Cady
  Elizabeth Cady Stanton and, 55–56

History of Woman Suffrage, The
  (coauthor with Stanton), 53

National Woman Suffrage
  Association, 46

Antony, Marc. *See* Cleopatra VII

Aquino, Benigno "Ninoy."
  See Aquino, Corazon

Aquino, Corazon, 147–150, 261
  as president of Philippines, 150

Argentina, 50, 109–113, 260

Armed Services Committee, 206

Auletes (Ptolemy XIII). *See* Cleopatra VII

Aung San Suu Kyi, 251–254, 262
  Anti-Fascist People's Freedom
    League, 252
  at Oxford University, 253
  Freedom from Fear (author), 253
  wins Nobel Peace Prize, 254

Australia, 15, 47, 263

Bandaranaike, Sirimavo, 92–95, 261
  as prime minister of Sri Lanka, 94, 95

Battle of Actium, 22

Baumfree, Isabella. *See* Truth, Sojourner

Beecher, Henry Ward, 46

Bhutto, Benazir, 15, 240–243, 261
    as political prisoner, 242
    as prime minister of Pakistan, 242,
        243
Bolivia, 260
Bondfield, Margaret, 44
Boxer, Barbara, 180, 188–191
    and Education Corps of Marin
        County, 189
    and Violence Against Women Act, 190
    as cochair of Military Reform
        Caucus, 190
    as president of Marin County Board
        of Supervisors, 189
    as U.S. Senator, 190
Boxer Rebellion, *See* Tz'u-hsi
Brundtland, Gro Harlem, 200–203
    as chairperson of United Nations
        World Commission on Environ-
        ment and Development, 202
    as head of World Health
        Organization, 202, 203
    as prime minister of Norway, 202
    election to Storting (parliament), 202
Byrne, Jane, 159–162
    as cochair of Cook County Democratic
        Central Committee, 161
    as John F. Kennedy campaign staffer,
        160
    as mayor of Chicago, 162

Caesar, Julius. *See* Cleopatra VII
de Calvo, Esther Neira, 50
Campbell, Kim, 236–239, 259

    as minister of Indian affairs and
        northern development, 238
    as prime minister of Canada, 238
    as Progressive Conservative Party
        leader, 238
Canada, 236–239, 259
Catherine the Great, 35–38, 261
    and government reform, 37
    as empress of Russia, 37, 38
    Peter III, emperor of Russia and, 37
    slavery and, 37–38
de Chamorro, Violeta Barrios, 14,
    131–134, 259–260
    as president of Nicaragua, 133, 134
    as publisher of *La Prensa*
        (newspaper), 132–133
    National Opposition Union and, 133
Charles, Mary Eugenia, 105–108, 260
    and Dominica Freedom Party, 107 108
    as prime minister of Dominica, 107,
        108
Cherokee Nation. *See* Mankiller, Wilma
    Pearl
China, 63–65, 261
Chisholm, Shirley, 118–120
    as candidate for president, 120
    election to New York State
        Assembly, 119
    election to U.S. Congress, 119, 120
    National Political Congress of Black
        Women, 120
Çiller, Tansu, 222–225, 261
    election as prime minister of Turkey,
        224
    True Path Party and, 223

Clement VII, 29
Cleopatra VII, 19–23, 262
   ascends throne of Egypt, 20
   Julius Caesar and, 22
   Marc Antony and, 22, 23
   Octavius and, 22–23
Clinton, Hillary Rodham, 226–230
   as chair of Task Force on National
      Health Care Reform, 230
   House of Representatives' Judiciary
      Committee, 228
   Olympia Snowe and, 206
   Patricia Schroeder and, 206
Columbus, Christopher, 27
Commission on Human Rights, 83
Connecticut War Manpower
   Commission, 103
Coppa, Minerva Bernardino, 50
Cresson, Edith, 163–167
   as head of Ministry of Agriculture,
      164
   as mayor of Thuré, 164
   as minister of trade and tourism, 165
   becomes prime minister of France,
      165
   Boris Yeltsin, president of Russia
      and, 166
   resignation of, 167
Crimean War, 60

Daley, Richard J. See Byrne, Jane
Dallas Committee for Peaceful
   Integration, 156
Declaration of Conscience, 84

Declaration of Sentiments, 52
Denmark, woman's suffrage in, 48
Dissawa, Sirimavo Ratwatte.
   See Bandaranaike, Sirimavo
Dominica. See Charles, Eugenia
Dominis, John, 67
Dreaver, Mary, 48

Edict of Tolerance, 30
Education Amendments of 1972, 207
Education Infrastructure Act, 195
Egypt, 49
Eighty Years and More (Stanton), 53
Environmental Protection Agency,
   212–213
Equal Rights Amendment (ERA), 137,
   207, 249
European Monetary System, 125

Fawcett, Millicent G., 44
Feinstein, Dianne, 15, 180, 184–187
   becomes mayor of San Francisco, 186
   becomes U.S. senator, 187
Ferdinand II. See Isabella I
Ferraro, Geraldine Anne, 16, 168–172
   and Special Victims Bureau, 169
   as vice-presidential candidate, 171
   Walter Mondale and, 170–171
Finland, woman's suffrage in, 48
Finnbogadottir, Vigdis, 140–142
   as director of Reykjavik Theatre
      Company, 141
   elected as president of Iceland, 142
foot binding. See Tz'u-hsi

Fourteenth Amendment, 55
France. *See* Cresson, Edith, and
    de Médicis, Catherine
Freedom from Fear (Aung San Suu Kyi),
    253
Freedom of Information Act, 117
French West Africa, woman's suffrage
    in, 48–49

Gage, Matilda Joslyn, 53
Ghana, woman's suffrage in, 48
Ghandi, Indira, 96–100, 261
    arrest of, 97
    assassination of, 100
    becomes prime minister of India, 99
    Jawaharlal Nehru and, 98
    Monkey Brigade, 97
Godwin, Mary Wollstonecraft, 42, 44
Government of Ireland Act, 256
Grasso, Ella, 101–104
    and Connecticut War Manpower
        Commission, 103
    becomes governor of Connecticut,
        104
Great Briain, 44, 46, 121–125
Greece. *See* ancient Greece

Haiti, 260
Hawaii, 66–69
Henry II. *See* de Médicis, Catherine
Hill, Anita, 181–183, 192, 194
History of Woman Suffrage, The
    (Stanton and Anthony), 53
Hughes, Dorothy Pitman, 249

Iceland, 48, 140–142
India, 49, 62, 96–100, 261
Inter-American Commission of
    Women, 50
Iran, 49
Ireland, 208–210, 244, 255–258
Isabella I, 24–27
    ascends throne of Spain, 26
    Christopher Columbus and, 27
    Spanish Inquisition and, 26–27
Israeli Proclamation of Independence, 90

John, Patrick, prime minister of
    Dominica, 107
Jordan, Barbara Charline, 173–175
    as Democratic Nation Convention
        keynote speaker, 175
    as Texas state senator, 174
    enters U.S. Congress, 174, 175

Kassebaum, Nancy, 143–146, 180
    becomes U.S. senator, 146
    Republican Majority Coalition and,
        146
Kinigi, Sylvie, 263
Kirkpatrick, Jeane, 126–130
    as U.S. ambassador to United
        Nations, 129–130
Kollontai, Aleksandra Mikhaylovna,
    70–73
    and Russian Social Democratic
        party, 73
    and Second International Communist
        Woman's Conference, 72

Kunin, Madeleine, 151–154
    elected as governor of Vermont, 153
    environmental laws and, 153

La Prensa (newspaper). See de
    Chamorro, Violeta Barrios
Latin America, 49–50, 259, 260
League of Women Voters, 81, 119, 152
Lebanon, 49
Liliuokalani, 66–69
    "Aloha Oe" (song), 69
    ascends throne of Hawaii, 68
    deposed from throne, 68
    John Dominis and, 67
Lutz, Bertha, 50
Lyons, Enid, 47

Maine, 84–87, 231–235
Mankiller, Wilma Pearl, 211–213
    and American Indian Movement,
        212
    becomes chief of Cherokee Nation,
        212
    Environmental Protection Agency
        and, 212–213
Marcos, Ferdinand. See Aquino,
    Corazon
Mary, Queen of Scots. See Stuart, Mary
matriarchal societies, 15
matrifocal societies, 18
McAliskey, Bernadette Devlin, 244,
        255–258
    becomes Northern Ireland's
        representative in British House

        of Commons, 257
    People's Democracy movement, 257
McCombs, Elizabeth, 48
de Médicis, Catherine, 28–31
    as regent, 30
    Edit of Tolerance and, 30
    Louvre Palace and, 31
    Peace of Saint-Germain and, 30
    St. Bartholomew's Day Massacre
        and, 30
    Tuileries gardens and, 31
Meir, Golda, 88–91
    as secretary general of Israeli Labor
        Party, 90
    becomes prime minister of Israel, 90
    World War II and, 90
Mexico, 50, 259
Mikulski, Barbara Ann, 176–179
    as member of Baltimore City
        Council, 178
    becomes U.S. senator, 178
Mondale, Walter. See Geraldine Ferraro
monotheistic religions, 18
Moseley-Braun, Carol, 180, 192–195
    as member of Illinois House of
        Representatives, 193
    Education Infrastructure Act and,
        195
    elected to U.S. Congress, 194
    Project Synergy and, 195
    United Daughters of the Confederacy
        and, 195
Mott, Lucretia, 46, 52
Murray, Pat, 180
Myanmar. See Aung San Suu Kyi

Narrative of Sojourner Truth, The (Truth), 40

National American Woman Suffrage Association, 46, 53

National Council for the Prevention of War, 77

National Labor Relations Board, 205

National Opposition Union, 133

National Political Congress of Black Women, 120

National Task Force on Equal Rights for Women, 207

National Union of Women's Suffrage Societies, 44

National Woman Suffrage Association, 46, 53, 57

National Women's Political Caucus, 117

New Jersey, 214–217

New York. *See* Anthony, Susan B.; Chisolm, Shirley; Stanton, Elizabeth Cady

New Zealand, 15, 47, 48, 263

Nicaragua. *See* de Chamorro, Violeta Barrios

Nineteenth Amendment, 46–47, 57

North Dallas Democratic Women Organization, 156

Norway, 48

O'Connor, Sandra Day, 14, 135–139
    becomes U.S. Supreme Court Justice, 138
    Equal Rights Amendment and, 137
    Ronald Reagan and, 137

Octavius. *See* Cleopatra VII

Orange Free State, 48

Pakistan. *See* Bhutto, Benazir

Panama, 50

Pascal-Trouillot, Ertha, 260

Peace of Saint-Germain, 30

Perón, Eva, 109–113
    and social programs in Argentina, 112
    political activities of, 110, 112
    voting rights and, 112

Perón, Isabel, 260

Peter III. *See* Catherine the Great

Philippines, 49. *See also* Aquino, Corazon de Piedra, Rosario Ibarra, 259

Poland. *See* Suchocka, Hanna

Poland: The Role of the Press in Political Change (Albright), 198

Privacy Act, 117

Project Synergy, 195

Ptolemy XII. *See* Cleopatra VII

Rankin, Jeanette, 74–78, 85
    election to U.S. Congress, 75
    Vietnam War and, 78
    World War I and, 75–77
    World War II and, 77, 78

religion
    authority of women in, 18
    monotheistic, 18

Republican Majority Coalition, 146

Revolution (newspaper), 53

Richards, Ann, 155–158
    Dallas Committee for Peaceful
        Integration and, 156
    election as governor of Texas, 158
    North Dallas Democratic Women
        Organization and, 156
Robinson, Mary, 208–210
    election as president of Ireland, 209
    election to Irish Parliament, 209
Roosevelt, Anna Eleanor, 12–13, 79–83
    activities with League of Women
        Voters, 81
    as chair of U.N. Commission on
        Human Rights, 83
    as radio broadcaster, 83
    "My Day" (newspaper column),
        82–83
    political and social welfare activities
        of, 81
Roosevelt, Franklin, 80
Roosevelt, Theodore, 80
Russia, 38, 72, 73, 261
Rwanda. *See* Uwilingiyimana, Agathe

San Francisco. *See* Boxer, Barbara;
    Feinstein, Dianne
Sauvé, Jeanne, 259
Schroeder, Patricia, 204–207
    election to U.S. Congress, 20
    Hillary Rodham Clinton and, 206
    National Labor Relations Board and,
        205
    National Task Force on Equal Rights
        for Women and, 207

Second International Communist
    Woman's Conference, 72
Senate Judiciary Committee, 180–181
Seneca Falls Convention, 52
slavery, 17, 37–39, 46, 52, 54
Smith, Margaret Chase, 84–87
    as presidential candidate, 86
    Declaration of Conscience and, 85
    enters U.S. Congress, 85
    Joseph McCarthy and, 86
Snowe, Olympia, 231–235
    as Congressional Caucus for
        Women's Issues cochair, 234
    enters Maine House of
        Representatives, 232
    enters U.S. Congress, 234
    Hillary Rodham Clinton and, 206
Spain. *See* Isabella I
Special Victims Bureau, 169
Sri Lanka. *See* Bandaranaike, Sirimavo
St. Bartholomew's Day Massacre, 30
Stanton, Elizabeth Cady, 46, 51–53
    as coauthor of Declaration of
        Sentiments, 52
    as coauthor, with Susan B. Anthony,
        of *History of Woman Suffrage, The*, 53
    as president of National American
        Woman Suffrage Association, 53
    at Seneca Falls Convention, 52
    Eighty Years and More (book), 53
    slavery and, 52
    Susan B. Anthony and, 55–56
    temperance movement and, 52
    Woman's Bible, The (book), 53
Stanton, Henry, 52

Steinem, Gloria, 247–250
    and work with Cesar Chavez, 249
    cofounds National Women's Political
        Caucus, 249
    founds *Ms.* Magazine, 249
Stone, Lucy, 46
Stuart, Mary, 32–34
    and Elizabeth I of England, 34
    ascends throne of Scotland, 33
    becomes queen of France, 33
    execution of, 34
Suchocka, Hanna, 218–221
    becomes prime minister of Poland,
        220
    election to Sejm (lower house of
        Polish parliament), 219

Tagney, Dorothy, 47
Tejada, Lidia Gueiler, 260
Temperance movement, 45–46, 52, 55
Texas. *See* Richards, Ann; Jordan, Barbara
Thailand, 49
Thatcher, Margaret, 121–125
    and Falkland Islands conflict, 123
    becomes prime minister of Great
        Britain, 122
    elected to British parliament, 122
    European Monetary System and, 125
    Ronald Reagan and, 123–124
Thomas, Clarence, 180–183, 192, 194
Truth, Sojourner, 39–41
    Civil War and, 40
    Narrative of Sojourner Truth, The
        (book), 40

Turkey, 49, 261. *See also* Çiller, Tansu
Tz'u-hsi, 63–65, 261
    becomes coregent of China, 64, 65
    Boxer Rebellion and, 65
    foot binding and, 64

United Nations, 15, 16, 129, 198, 199, 202
U.S. Congress, 74–78, 84–87, 144, 178, 180,
    183, 187, 190, 192–195, 231–235
U.S. Supreme Court, 14, 135–139, 180
Uwilingiyimana, Agathe, 263

Victoria I, 58–62
    and Victorian Age, 62
    creates Victoria Cross medal, 60
    Crimean War and, 60
    marries Albert, Prince of Saxe-
        Coburg, 60
    de Vidal Urdenata, Isabel, 50
Vietnam War, 78, 116, 205
Vindication of the Rights of Women, A
    (Godwin), 42, 44
Violence Against Women Act, 190
voting rights. *See* woman's suffrage

Women's Environmental Development
    Organization (WEDO), 117
Whitman, Christine Todd, 214–217
    election as governor of New Jersey,
        216
    election to Somerset County Board
        of Chosen Freeholders, 215–216

Woman's Bible, The (Stanton), 53
Woman's State Temperance Society of
    New York, 55
woman's suffrage, 42–50, 244
    Africa, 48
    American Woman Suffrage
        Association, 57
    Argentina, 50
    British suffrage movement, 44
    Denmark, 48
    Egypt, 49
    Finland, 48
    French West Africa, 48–49
    Ghana, 48
    Iceland, 48
    India, 49
    Iran, 49
    Latin America, 49–50
    Lebanon, 49
    Mexico, 50

    Middle East, 49
    National Union of Women's Suffrage
        Societies, 44
    National Woman Suffrage
        Association, 46, 57
    Norway, 48
    Orange Free State, 48
    Panama, 50
    Philippines, 49
    Thailand, 49
    Turkey, 49
    Wyoming Territory, 53
Women's Congress for a Healthy
    Planet, 117
Women's Labor Council of the
    Histadrut, 90
World Health Organization, 202

Zionism, 89

Photo Credits

Photographs ©: AP/Wide World Photos: 6, 7, 8, 9, 92, 98, 105, 111, 114, 151, 155, 200, 218, 222, 245, 8, 184, 128, cover background, 145, cover bottom right, 3, 8, 173, 9, 240,159, 233, 166, 7, 147, 170, 131, 124, 8, 204, 7, 143 229; Archive Photos: 5, 35; Art Resource: 5, 28, 21, 32 (Giraudon); Barbara Boxer, U.S. Senate: 8, 188; Corbis-Bettmann: cover bottom left square, 3, 5, 6, 19, 24, 39, 43, 51, 54, 56, 63, 66, 247; Culver Pictures: 78, 82; Courtesy of Department of State, U.S.A.: cover top right square, 3, 8, 196; Embassy of Ireland: 9, 208; Franklin D. Roosevelt Library: back cover center right, 6, 79; Gamma-Liaison: back cover top right (James Schnepf), cover top left square, 3, 7, 109 (Raphael Woolman), 8, 181 (D. Yee), 9, 211 (James Schnepf), 182 (Brad Markel), back cover center left, 9, 226 (Diane Walker); Jay Mallin: 8, 176, 192; Kim Campbell: 9, 236; New York Public Library Picture Collection: 61; Reuters/Corbis-Bettmann: 7, 8, 9, 135, 163, 251; Senator Olympia Snowe: 9, 231; State of New Jersey Office of the Governor: 9, 214; UPI/Corbis-Bettmann: back cover top left, back cover bottom center, 6, 7, 8, 10, 45, 58, 70, 72, 74, 84, 96, 101, 118, 121, 126, 138, 140, 168, 255.

About the Author

Charles Gulotta was born and raised in New York City. He met his wife, Maria, while both were living in Connecticut. They recently moved to an old farmhouse on Prince Edward Island, Canada, with their children, Meaghan, Allison, and Shaun. Gulotta has also authored *500 SAT Words, and How to Remember Them Forever!* and *100 SAT Math Tips, and How to Master Them Now!*.